# EQUINE NUTRITION

 PELHAM HORSEMASTER SERIES

# EQUINE NUTRITION

A. C. Leighton Hardman

**PELHAM BOOKS**

First published in Great Britain by
PELHAM BOOKS LTD
44 Bedford Square
London WC1B 3DP
1980
Reprinted 1982, 1984 and 1985

British Library Cataloguing in Publication Data

Leighton Hardman, Ann Catherine
    Equine nutrition – (Horsemaster).
    1. Horses – Feeding and feeds
    I. Title    II. Series
    636.1'08'52          SF285.5

ISBN 0 7207 1244 0

Typeset by Cambrian Typesetters, Farnborough
Printed in Great Britain by
Hollen Street Press, Slough

# CONTENTS

# ACKNOWLEDGEMENTS

I wish to thank Mr J. L. Lees of the Department of Agriculture, University of Wales and Sidney W. Ricketts, BSc, BVSc, FRCVS for checking the manuscript and for their invaluable help and advice.

Also Geoffrey Francis, BSc of Cambridge, for his helpful suggestions, explanations and patience over the years and without whose tuition this book could not have been written.

For the data on the mares my thanks are due to the owners, managers and staff of the three Newmarket studs who put up with me and my tapemeasure for so long. I am most grateful to Dr Jeffcott and his staff for allowing me to measure weighed horses and ponies at the Equine Research Station.

I also wish to thank Liam Wilson of Pegus Foods Ltd. for having samples of hay and other foodstuffs analysed for the project.

I am indebted to the following publications and their editors for permission to use copyright material and ideas: National Research Council, Washington D.C., National Institute of Agricultural Botany, Cambridge and National Institute for Research in Dairying, Shinfield.

My thanks to John Murray of Peter Hand (GB) Ltd for supplying the data for the guide to the nutritive value of foodstuffs. Also to Robin McEnery, MRCVS, for the X-ray photographs, to GHL Products, Crewe, who kindly provided the picture of a weighing machine and to Geoffrey Wragg for weight details of horses in training.

Finally, I sincerely appreciate the skilful work of my publishers.

Ann Leighton Hardman
Newmarket

# 1 Condition Scoring and Weight Estimation

Nutrition is intrinsically linked with health, and has a profound effect on it at all stages in the horse's life. These days foodstuffs and veterinary bills represent a large percentage of the cost of keeping a horse. A knowledge of the principles of feeding and their effect on health will undoubtedly save the reader money.

Nutrition affects well-being and this in turn affects growth, as well as reproductive and athletic performance. The link can be summed up briefly as follows:

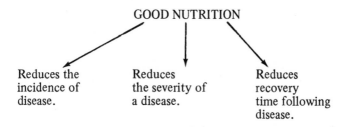

GOOD NUTRITION

Reduces the incidence of disease.

Reduces the severity of a disease.

Reduces recovery time following disease.

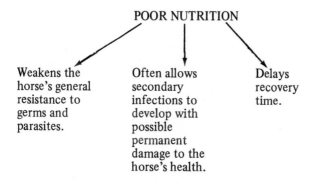

POOR NUTRITION

Weakens the horse's general resistance to germs and parasites.

Often allows secondary infections to develop with possible permanent damage to the horse's health.

Delays recovery time.

Correct feeding is based on the horse's optimum live-weight, which is related to condition. Horses and ponies are individual in their response to feeds and feeding practices, so it is not possible to rely on rigid ration scales. Those who feed horses must be able to assess condition, as without this information it is impossible to balance dietary energy and feed correctly. Most text-books tell you that the best way to gauge the energy level of a ration is to examine the horse's condition and adjust the diet accordingly. Too much energy will make a horse fat and too little will keep him thin; either way performance will be affected.

The condition of an animal is related to the amount of fatty tissue under the skin in certain areas – this is an indication of the animal's body reserves of energy and is a valuable guide to management. Since there is a relationship between condition and peak performance in all spheres, a simple method of assessing condition accurately and quickly is important. One such method is known as condition scoring[1]. This assesses the amount of subcutaneous fat over the hindquarters by applying a scale of points from 0 (very poor) to 5 (grossly fat), with half scores between, giving an 11-point scale. The pelvis score is used and adjusted if it differs greatly from the backbone and rib area and base of neck scores. It is unlikely that all three scores will be different, and in practice at least two are always the same.

**Method of scoring**: It is surprising just how easily the eye can be deceived, so examination must also include manual inspection. This gives better results than visual assessment alone, due to variations in conformation and thickness of coat. For consistency the same hand should be used throughout.

(1) Stand directly behind the horse. Note the amount of flesh covering the pelvis and top of the quarters. If the horse is in poor condition you will note a deep cavity under the tail, the bone structure will be clearly

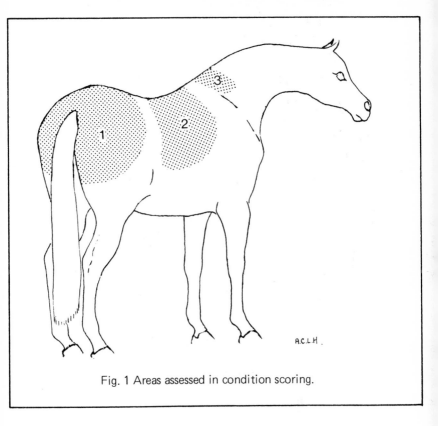

Fig. 1 Areas assessed in condition scoring.

visible and the flanks will appear hollow, with little muscle between the hind legs. If the skin is drawn tightly over the pelvis and the animal appears emaciated, score 0. If the skin is supple, score 1.

If you can still feel the pelvis but all the bones are covered and their angles look rounded, the horse is in moderate or good condition. Depending on the amount of fatty tissue felt under the skin, score 2 or 3.

If on the other hand the pelvis is buried in rolls of fat and no part of the bone structure can be felt and there is a 'gutter' running down the mid-line of the back to the root of the tail, the horse is fat. The difference between fat and grossly fat depends on the amount of fatty tissue present. Score 4 or 5.

(2) Score the backbone and rib area in the same way. The bones should just be covered and the individual processes of the spine should not be visible to the eye (this would mean that the horse was in poor condition). If the processes and ribs are covered but can be felt with the fingers then the animal is in good condition. A hollow or 'gutter' running down the horse's back along the line of the backbone is a sign of overweight. The amount of excess fat present can be gauged by feeling for the spine with the fingers — if the bony processes cannot be felt at all, the animal must be considered grossly fat.

(3) Score the base of the neck. Stand by the horse's shoulder, note the shape of the neck — an ewe neck may, but does not always, indicate poor condition — sometimes it is just a conformation fault. A marked crest is usually a sign of overweight, except in male horses when it is synonymous with masculinity. Using the fingers and thumb of the hand used previously, feel the amount of muscle at the base of the neck just in front of the withers. A horse in poor condition will feel narrow and slack, one in good condition will feel wide and firm. Assess the score as before.

Adjust the pelvis score by half a point if it differs from the back or neck scores by one point or more. If the back and neck scores differ by an equal amount either side of the pelvis score, leave the latter unaltered.

The adjusted pelvis score is the *condition score.* Scores should be taken weekly to show changes in condition, so that the diet can be altered if necessary.

Having obtained the horse's condition score, its optimum score must be established. This is affected by conformation, class of horse, use, degree of fitness etc. Horses in training normally have an individual score which is related to peak performance. Regular liveweight records will pinpoint this relationship. Weighing

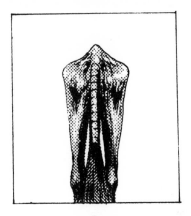

Score                      **0**

Condition                  **VERY POOR**

Pelvis area                Deep cavity under tail and either side of croup. Pelvis looks and feels angular. Skin drawn tightly over pelvis with no tissue detectable between.

Back and ribs              Individual processes of backbone sharp to touch and very clearly defined. Skin drawn tightly over clearly defined ribs. Animal appears emaciated.

Neck area                  Ewe neck, very narrow and slack at base.

Score                      **1**

Condition                  **POOR**

Pelvis area                Croup and pelvis well defined. No fatty tissue present but skin is supple. Deep depression under tail.

Back and ribs              Individual processes of the backbone sharp to touch and clearly defined. Ribs clearly visible.

Neck area                  Ewe neck, narrow and slack at base.

| Score | 2 |
| --- | --- |
| Condition | MODERATE |
| Pelvis area | Croup well defined but some fatty tissue felt under the skin. Pelvis felt easily. Slight cavity under the tail. |
| Back and ribs | Backbone just covered. Individual processes not apparent but can easily be felt with pressure. Ribs just visible. |
| Neck area | Narrow but firm. |

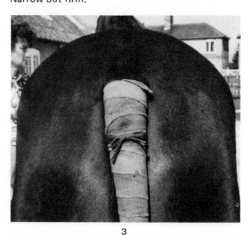

| Score | 3 |
| --- | --- |
| Condition | GOOD |
| Pelvis area | Fatty tissue covering whole area giving a rounded appearance without any 'gutter'. Skin appears smooth but pelvis easily felt. |
| Back and ribs | Vertebrae well covered but without a 'gutter'. Backbone easily felt with pressure. Ribs just covered. |
| Neck area | Firm, but with no crest except for stallions. |

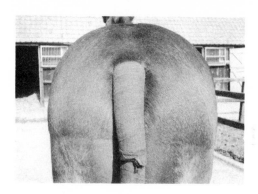

| Score | 4 |
|---|---|
| Condition | FAT |
| Pelvis area | Pelvis buried in soft fatty tissue. 'Gutter' to root of tail. Pelvis felt only with firm pressure. |
| Back and ribs | 'Gutter' along length of backbone. Ribs well covered by fatty tissue. Bone structure felt only with firm pressure. |
| Neck area | Wide and firm, with folds of fatty tissue present. Slight crest even in mares. |

| Score | 5 |
|---|---|
| Condition | GROSSLY FAT |
| Pelvis area | Pelvis buried in fatty tissue. Deep 'gutter' to root of tail. Skin distended. No part of pelvis felt even with firm pressure. |
| Back and ribs | Deep 'gutter' along backbone. Ribs buried in fatty tissue. Bone structure cannot be felt. Back more like a table. |
| Neck area | Very wide and firm, with folds of fatty tissue present. Marked crest even in mares. |

| Pelvis score | Back score | Difference from pelvis score | Neck score | Difference from pelvis score | Adjustment | CONDITION SCORE |
|---|---|---|---|---|---|---|
| $4\frac{1}{2}$ | 3 | $-1\frac{1}{2}$ | $4\frac{1}{2}$ | None | $-\frac{1}{2}$ | 4 |
| 0 | 1 | $+1$ | 0 | None | $+\frac{1}{2}$ | $\frac{1}{2}$ |
| 3 | 4 | $+1$ | 2 | $-1$ | None | 3 |
| 2 | $1\frac{1}{2}$ | $-\frac{1}{2}$ | $1\frac{1}{2}$ | $-\frac{1}{2}$ | None | 2 |

Fig. 2 Adjustment of pelvis score.

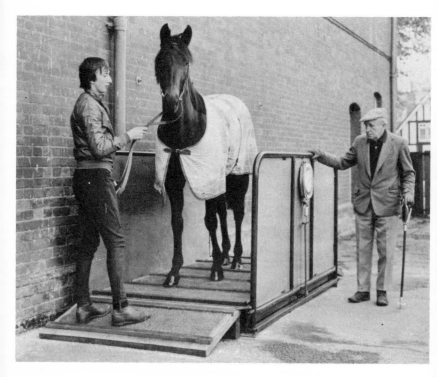

Weighing a horse using a weighbridge.

is also essential when a new horse first arrives in the yard. Although scoring is the best method of recording the link between dietary energy and condition it cannot give an accurate estimate of the quantity of food the horse should receive. This is based on liveweight. Adult horses consume 2.5 per cent of their body weight in food per day, broodmares and youngstock 3 per cent.

There are two ways of assessing liveweight – either the horse is placed on a suitable weighbridge, such as the one shown, or its liveweight can be estimated from heart girth and length measurements, taken with a 10 m (33 ft) fibre tapemeasure. The horse's length is measured from the point of shoulder to the point of

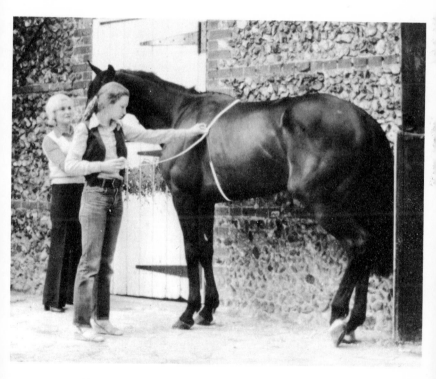

How to estimate weight using the tapemeasure.

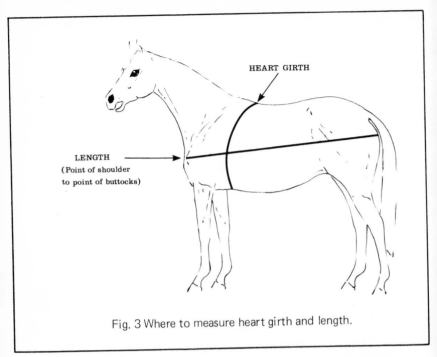

Fig. 3 Where to measure heart girth and length.

buttocks and girth circumference at the moment when the horse has exhaled. The tape should be held tightly. Measurements are recorded in inches.

The formula recommended was adapted from those given by Milner and Hewitt (1969)[2] and Ensminger (1977)[3] and is based on the mean liveweights of 209 horses, cobs and ponies, from Shires to Shetlands[4].

$$\frac{girth^2 \times length}{y} = \text{estimated weight (lb.)}$$

Estimated weight (lb.) x 0.45 = estimated weight (kg.)

The non-adjusted factors y for use in the formula can be found on page 106. For greater accuracy use the table on page 107 which gives adjusted factors y according to condition score.

When investigating the relationship between girth and length measurements and recorded body weight, it was felt that either the amount of bone a horse had or his body condition might influence factor y. Bone, height, skinfold thickness and condition score were therefore recorded. No trend was observed for bone, height or skinfold thickness but a linear relationship was seen in the case of condition score. Predicted values were calculated for the difference between factor y and group mean for every value of condition score for each class of animal. Regression lines were drawn. The $r^2$ values were calculated and confirmed the high level of prediction which can be achieved using weight estimation formulae.

REFERENCES

1 Horse condition scoring is adapted from NIRD (National Institute for Research in Dairying) Paper No. **4468**.
2 Milner and Hewitt *Am. Vet. J.,* **10**, 314 (1969).
3 Ensminger, M. E. *Horses and Horsemanship,* 5th edition (1977).
4 Leighton Hardman A.C. Study of the Relationship between Body Measurement, Body Condition and Liveweight of the Horse (1981).

# 2 The Effect of Environment on Dietary Energy Requirement

A horse's living conditions are normally determined by man. The best environment allows the greatest expression of inherited potential, while poor conditions create stress factors. The effect of housing and environment on nutrition and health is therefore an important study. These factors are closely inter-related.

*Environment* can be defined as *Accommodation + Nutrition + Management + Disease.*

All animals regulate body temperature by heat exchange with the surrounding atmosphere. The environment, therefore, has a major influence on the amount of heat lost by the horse. Heat comes either directly or indirectly from food, so there is a definite relationship between environment and food energy utilisation. In cold weather, there is a reduction in the amount of energy available for more productive activities such as work and growth unless body heat is regulated sufficiently. On the other hand, when environmental temperature is high, heat production decreases until a point is reached when the horse cannot reduce it any further; beyond this point body temperature rises and the animal becomes distressed. Between these two extremes there is an area known as the thermal neutral zone, where heat production is minimal, a maximum amount of energy remains available for useful activities and little is wasted. Maintenance requirements are based on this state and must be adjusted for other conditions.

*Heat loss* is reduced by constriction of the peripheral circulation; lack of sweating (evaporative heat loss) and by a winter coat.

*Heat production* is proportional to body weight and comes from basal metabolism + energy released during work or exercise, including shivering + heat increment of digestion, especially caecal microbial digestion. Hence the value of digestible fibre, such as hay, in cold weather. Animals on a generous diet produce more heat and can therefore withstand colder conditions. The larger the animal the greater the surface area exposed to the atmosphere and the greater the heat loss. This is the theory behind metabolic body size (weight), which states that surface area is proportional to the three-quarters power of liveweight ($W^{0.75}$). (See Fig. 12 on page 61.) This factor is used in dietary energy requirement calculations.

Subcutaneous fatty tissue acts as a thermal insulation against cold. These layers of fat normally increase as the animal grows, so an adult pony of the same height as a horse foal will withstand lower environmental temperatures before body heat loss takes place. Similarly, newborn foals are most prone to body heat loss: the percentage of subcutaneous fat increases linearly from 2.5 per cent at birth to 15 per cent at maturity in light breeds[1] and from 6.1 per cent to 14.6 per cent in draft breeds[2].

Lack of insulation is therefore a reason why horses in poor condition have a lowered resistance to cold, wet and windy conditions. It takes a diet with a higher energy density to get them back into good condition, since you have to feed for maintenance + weight gain + increased energy loss. This is usually expressed as, say, 1.2 x M (where M = maintenance). Similarly, animals in fat condition will require a sub-maintenance diet of, say, 0.8 M to get them back into good condition.

Insulation is normally provided by nature and/or man. The horse grows a thick coat in winter and has a shorter finer coat in summer. The thicker and longer the coat the greater the insulation against body heat loss. The coat contains grease which further increases insulation mainly by keeping the horse's skin dry. Horses at grass should therefore not be groomed to remove grease from their coats. A surface shine can be obtained in most cases with a damp body brush and coarse stable rubber. Foals are born with thick woolly coats, and do not lose them until they are about three months old and have had time to build up reserves of subcutaneous body fat.

In order to conserve dietary energy, it is customary to stable horses during colder weather and/or when necessary to provide them with clothing. Rugs and blankets add to the horse's natural insulation and help to reduce unnecessary heat loss when there is a drop in environmental temperature. New Zealand waterproof rugs are often used for horses turned out in cold, wet, windy weather. When horses and ponies are clipped, rugs and blankets are provided to replace the natural insulation which has been removed, otherwise excessive heat loss takes place and expensive food energy will be utilised to keep the horse warm.

When man restricts a horse's freedom to choose its environment, it is essential to study its requirements in order to make the best use of dietary energy.

Wild horses and ponies automatically find the most sheltered areas of their terrain in bad weather. Groups of animals tend to huddle together and so reduce the surface area exposed to the atmosphere and therefore heat loss. Since other horses are normally confined to a limited area, shelter should be provided for them particularly in bad weather. This normally takes the form of stabling or field shelters, and paddocks affording the best natural shelter and driest ground should be used wherever possible.

The amount and quality of fresh herbage declines during the winter months, so the naturally available level of feeding drops. When dietary energy is low, heat production declines: the individual is unable to keep itself warm, draws on its fat reserves and loses weight. When supplementary feeding is offered heat production rises.

Housed stock too may be subject to stress factors. These include:

*Air temperature* — for comfort this should not be allowed to fall below 40°F (4°C). Newborn foals should be maintained at a temperature of 70°-75°F (21°-24°C) until they have dried out.

*Humidity* — for winter 80-85 per cent relative humidity is advised, but this would be difficult to achieve in high rainfall areas. Good ventilation at all times is the most important factor.

*Air velocity* — cold windy conditions and draughts increase heat loss, therefore ventilation in buildings must be draught-free but with sufficient air flow to ensure that there is no condensation moisture or odour in the stables. Inadequate ventilation is a predisposing cause of respiratory virus infections. Good ventilation can only be achieved if there is a satisfactory air inlet and outlet. This is usually done by opening loose-box half-doors, barn doors and windows — these should be of the hopper type to carry the air up over the horses' backs. Outlets must be installed on the ridge of the building to create adequate movement of air. In hot weather extractor fans are necessary in American barn type buildings.

*Insulation* — governs condensation moisture and atmospheric temperature in a building. This is the reason why animals always tend to 'do' better in stone or brick buildings than wooden ones; in the latter, roof and wall linings should be at least two inches thick.

*Bedding* — the deciding factors are the floor and the type, quantity and state of the bedding. Well-drained and therefore dry insulated floors give the best results. When a horse is lying down up to 20 per cent of his body may be in contact with the ground at any one time, and the type of floor and bedding used determines the amount of conductive heat loss. Scant bedding on an uninsulated, damp floor will result in the greatest heat loss. Free-draining slatted floors, used without bed-

Small area of the floor only bedded.

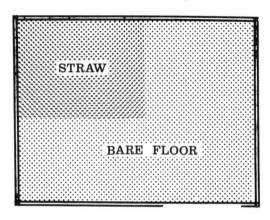

These two methods of bedding may give a difference of as much as 10°C. in the atmospheric temperature of the loose-box.

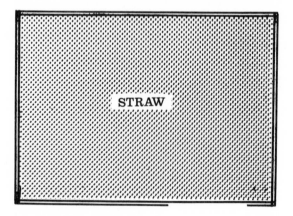

Completely bedded floor area.

Fig. 4 The effect of bedding on heat conservation.

ding, will produce lower atmospheric temperatures than a completely bedded floor area. A deep straw bed covering the whole floor is the warmest of all and therefore conserves most dietary energy.

Other stress factors associated with bedding include mucking-out efficiency and the level of ammonia, as well as of dust and mould spores in the bedding material and atmosphere. The latter cause such conditions as guttural pouch mycosis (fungal infection of the guttural pouch), broken-wind, and fungal infections of the genital tract including fungal abortions.

*Light* — for maximum health animals require fresh air and light. Optimum window space is considered to be not less than one square foot per thirty square feet of floor area. A 60-watt bulb gives sufficient light in a standard twelve-foot-square loose-box, but this should be increased to 200 watts for foaling boxes.

*Floor area* — loose-boxes should be twelve feet square, but sixteen square feet should be allowed for

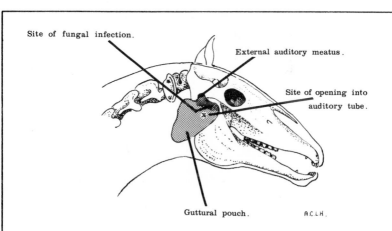

Fig. 5 Fungal infection of the guttural pouch (guttural pouch mycosis).

foaling boxes. Loose housing should allow a minimum area of one hundred and fifty square feet per animal.

Where horses are stabled under one roof, either in loose-boxes as in the American barn system or loose housed, heat dissipation from the animals may be enough to raise environmental temperature by several degrees. Conversely, when one animal is placed on its own in a large building in cold weather, for instance if the horse is in a twelve-foot-square loose-box in an otherwise empty American barn, it may be necessary to rug it and/or raise the atmospheric temperature of the building to 40°F (4°C), to prevent unnecessary body heat loss.

*Subclinical disease* — these are conditions giving symptoms of ill health so slight that they may escape the notice of all but the most vigilant owner. Subclinical disease affects metabolism and performance. Loose-boxes must be pressure- or steam-cleaned annually, and rested for as long as possible between animals. If not, a gradual disease build-up tends to occur until infection attacks every susceptible new horse coming into the yard and may even sweep through the whole yard. Paddocks must similarly be rested to minimise subclinical parasitic infections, which also affect food utilisation. Veterinary advice should be taken on such matters if necessary.

In conclusion, to counteract the effect of adverse climatic conditions and associated loss of dietary energy, action should be taken to:

  (i) increase the maintenance energy value of the diet;
 (ii) provide field shelters or house the stock in well insulated and ventilated buildings;
(iii) use the most sheltered paddocks and the driest ground preferably with a southern aspect;
 (iv) provide extra clothing;
  (v) make structural changes to the buildings according to prevailing economic circumstances;

(vi) consider the siting and aspect of new buildings in order to counter the effects of prevailing wind and weather and take advantage of sunshine and shelter.

## REFERENCES

1 NRC *Nutrient Requirements of Horses* National Research Council, Washington D.C. **6**, 4 (1978).
2 Martin-Rosset, W., *et al* 'Relative Growth of Different Organs, Tissues and Body Regions in the Foal from Birth to 30 Months'. 1979 Annual Meeting of the European Association for Animal Production, Harrogate.

# 3 The Horse's Protein Requirement

Youngstock and mares in the last ninety days of gestation and during lactation have a critical requirement for
protein quality. The quality of protein in a horse's diet
is related to the amino acids it contains. Amino acids are
the 'building blocks' from which proteins are made up,
and about twenty-five of these have been identified as
chemical compounds. The number present in a particular protein varies from two or three, as in gelatine, to
upwards of twelve or fifteen. The proportions vary considerably and farm feeds generally contain more than
one type of protein. A mixture of foods is therefore
likely to include a wide range of amino acids. Mature
horses do not have a critical requirement for amino
acids except perhaps under stress conditions. Young
growing animals and broodmares in the last ninety days
of gestation and during lactation do have a more deman-
ding pattern of amino acid requirements. Some ten or
twelve of these are thought of as essential in the diet, but
the other twelve or so can be produced by horses over
seven months old from the surplus of other amino acids
commonly present in a good diet.

A useful way to visualise a correct balance of essential
amino acids in a ration is to imagine that you are covering a bathroom or kitchen wall with a regular design of
multi-coloured tiles. The finished pattern represents the
balanced ration, so if only one tile is missing the effect
will be spoilt — i.e. the ration will be unbalanced. When
designing such a pattern an estimate can be made of the
numbers of tiles of each colour which will be needed and
these can be thought of as the theoretical requirement
for the job. If the cost per tile is known, then the least
cost of materials can be worked out. Unfortunately tiles
are usually sold in packets and allowance must also be
made for imperfections and wastage. As a consequence

the quantities needed in practice are more than the original calculation.

A similar concept applies to horse feeding, in that generally speaking practical diets should contain a modest safety margin of protein to ensure that there is no dietary burden on animals during stress conditions, e.g. cold, wet, windy weather or those stated in Chapter 4, pages 40–41. Diets rarely if ever contain the exact quantities of amino acids needed by an animal, so that extra protein is commonly fed to ensure an adequate level of the amino acids in shortest supply.

The *quantity* of protein needed by an animal is linked to several factors which include:

> Physiological performance – e.g. growth rate, stage of pregnancy, milk yield. This is by far the most important factor.
>
> Physical performance – e.g. amount of work being done, size of animal.
>
> Environmental conditions – e.g. housed or out wintered, amount of energy in the diet.

The *percentage* of protein needed is affected by:

> Dry matter intake – i.e. the appetite of the animal.
>
> Costiveness of the diet – i.e. rate of passage of the food.
>
> Energy density of the ration.

In the case of animals which have a critical requirement for amino acids one must also consider:

> The *quality* of protein, i.e. amino acid composition.

It is known that the value of proteins can be altered by physical factors, so that in practice we speak of *allowances* of protein for livestock. These allowances contain modest safety margins and apply to the average animal. In most cases this proves to be satisfactory, but in statistical terms some five to ten per cent of the animal population could still be underfed at the minimum allowance. Hence the wisdom of feeding horses as individuals.

The quality and percentage protein of a ration is

directly related to the type of foods it contains and their physical treatment.

An optimum ratio exists between protein and energy for all rations. The correct ratio maximises energy utilisation. A protein deficiency decreases energy utilisation and so increases the weight of food required per kg gain. Similarly, increasing the energy density of a ration automatically increases protein requirement.

All farm foods contain protein as well as energy, minerals and vitamins. Proportions vary: concentrate foods containing more than 35 per cent protein are high-protein; 20-35 per cent are medium-protein and those containing less than 20 per cent are low-protein.

When given free access to various foods, horses will usually select those with higher protein values. For example, 20 per cent crude protein lucerne meal is preferred to 16 per cent crude protein lucerne meal, and high-quality hay to poor-quality. This should be borne in mind when feeding poor eaters.

Protein supplements most commonly used in horse rations include:

Solvent extracted soyabean
    meal .................. 45% crude protein
Dried skimmed milk powder ... 37% crude protein
High-grade white fish meal .... 70% crude protein
Whole linseed ............. 26% crude protein

Low-protein foods make up the largest part of any mix and include:

Oats...................... 11% crude protein
Bran ..................... 17% crude protein
Barley .................... 11% crude protein
Flaked maize............... 11% crude protein
Sugar beet pulp ............ 10% crude protein

In order to balance a diet the amount and protein value of a mix for any class of horse depends on the protein value of bulky foods available. Hay is the bulky food of choice, and is therefore the key to good horse feeding.

Dry bulky foods usually contain less than 12 per cent crude protein:

Barn-dried hay:
| | |
|---|---|
| 1st quality | 12-13% crude protein |
| 2nd quality | 10% crude protein |
| 3rd quality | 6-8% crude protein |

Field-cured hay:
| | |
|---|---|
| Italian ryegrass | 3-6% crude protein |
| Perennial ryegrass | 5-8% crude protein |
| Clover mix (leafy) | 10-12% crude protein |

Green foods lie between dry bulky foods and protein concentrates, and with artificial drying they lose little of their feeding value:

| | |
|---|---|
| Dried grass | 12-18% crude protein |
| Dried lucerne | 14-22% crude protein |

Heat treatment of protein concentrates can affect their amino acid composition. Overheated hay is similarly affected.

Weather conditions during the growing season and at harvest affect both the quantity and quality of protein. Other factors with similar effects include storage conditions – e.g. weathering, rain and damp conditions or old age producing rancidity – and infestation with mites or contamination by vermin.

In chemical terms proteins are unique in that they contain nitrogen. This fact distinguishes them from fats, sugars and starches, which consist only of carbon, hydrogen and oxygen. The nitrogen in proteins is always present in identifiable groups combined with hydrogen ($NH_2$ groups). Protein molecules are very complex and besides carbon, hydrogen and oxygen may also contain sulphur, as in the amino acids methionine and cystine. The proportion of nitrogen present varies among the proteins but an average figure is 16 per cent. When determining the amount of protein in a feed, a chemist will estimate its nitrogen content and multiply the figure by 6.25 (this factor is 100 divided by 16). This is termed *crude protein* or *total protein.*

The term *digestible protein* may be used to describe the amount of dietary protein which is digested by an animal. Experimentally it can be measured by deducting the crude protein content of the dung from the crude protein content of the food eaten by the animal.

The digestibility factor of protein in farm foods can vary considerably, and is highest in fresh grass at early growth stage (85 per cent). In cereals and concentrates

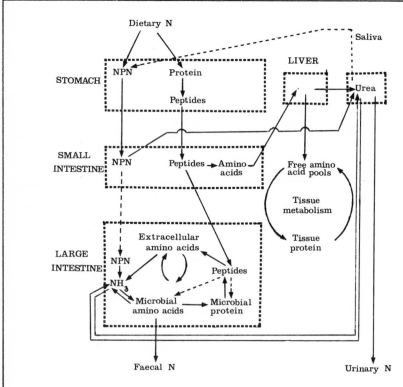

Fig. 6 Nitrogen digestion in the horse.

it is 75-80 per cent, in good hay 60 per cent, in weathered hay 40 per cent. Therefore the nature of the hay has a double effect on the degree of protein supplement needed to balance a ration – that is crude protein content and crude protein digested.

Protein is converted into amino acids and absorbed from the small intestine. Any peptides not split into amino acids pass down into the large intestine and are converted into microbial protein in the mature horse. In the young horse they are not utilised -- therefore foals up to seven months old should receive diets containing only high-grade protein. A daily supply of dietary protein is essential for all horses. Although some amino acids are stored in the liver, this in no way compares with the body's ability to store carbohydrates and fats. There is a constant turnover of protein from tissue, most of the 'new' protein going to replace 'old' protein and not increase muscle.

Synthetic amino acids such as lysine and methionine are sometimes used in horse rations as protein sparing factors.

The main reasons for this are:

(1) When using natural protein sources it is often necessary to use higher levels of protein than are absolutely essential to ensure that no one amino acid is in short supply. This can lead to initial digestive upsets.

(2) The better-quality protein foods are often the most expensive, and this can seriously affect the cost of a ration.

Non-protein nitrogen, such as urea, can be used in the diets of mature horses and ponies to supplement a low-protein ration[1]. Dietary urea is absorbed from the small intestine and not utilised for protein synthesis until secreted into the lumen of the large intestine, hydrolysed to ammonia and synthesised into microbial protein.

Where valuable stock are concerned, feeding urea cannot be justified. Very high levels of dietary urea are known to produce ammonia toxicity and death[2]. Levels normally recommended for beef cattle are unlikely to harm adult horses. Urea should not be fed to foals and yearlings under a year old.

**Warning:** Romensin (Monensin-sodium) is sometimes included in cattle fattening rations. It alters rumen fermentation, producing faster weight gains at the recommended level. If included in quantities above those detailed, it upsets digestion and causes weight loss. Cattle feed containing Romensin has been known to cause death when fed to horses.

A protein deficiency and lack of dietary energy normally occur together – the latter, coupled with depressed appetite symptoms, causes loss of weight.

A modest excess of dietary protein has no detrimental effect on the horse. The old idea that excess protein was harmful to horses was shown to be incorrect when vitamin $B_{12}$ was discovered. The symptoms noted were due to vitamin $B_{12}$ deficiency[3]. This vitamin is necessary for protein utilisation and as the protein density of a ration increases so the need for vitamin $B_{12}$ rises. Therefore, if vitamin $B_{12}$ is adequate there should be no harmful effect from the added protein. Excess protein is broken down and used as an additional source of energy.

REFERENCES

1 Frape, D. L. and Boxall, R. C. 'Some Nutritional Problems of the Horse and their Possible Relationship to those of other Herbivores' *Equine Vet. J.* **6**, 2.
2 NRC *Nutrient Requirements of Horses* National Research Council, Washington D.C. **6**, 4 (1978).
3 Cunha, Tony J. *Horse Feeding and Nutrition*, pub. Academic Press (1980).

# 4 The Role of Vitamins in Horse Feeding

Most of the work on vitamins has been carried out since 1911, when Casimir Funk first gave these vital food accessories the name vit*amine*. However, their role in preventing certain diseases had been appreciated for several hundred years before then. For instance, way back in 1753 a British naval physician published a treatise on scurvy and how it could be prevented by eating salads and fruit. Cod liver oil was also recognised as containing some factor which prevented rickets.

Vitamins are organic compounds which perform essential functions in the body but are only needed in very small amounts. Since they all perform different functions, it is important that an adequate supply of each one is available. They are essential for the growth and health of all horses and ponies.

The following are the essential vitamins:

*Water-soluble vitamins:*
(not stored by the body in
   significant amounts)
Vitamin C
B-complex vitamins:
   Thiamin
   Riboflavin
   Niacin
   Pantothenic acid
   $B_6$ and $B_{12}$
   Choline
   Inositol
   Biotin
   Folacin (Folic acid)
   Aminobenzoic acid

*Fat-soluble vitamins:*
(stored to some extent
   in the body)
Vitamin A
Vitamin D
Vitamin E
Vitamin K

Adult horses are able to synthesise many of the vitamins providing certain compounds, known as precursors, are present in the diet or synthesis is carried out by gut microbes in the large intestine.

*Vitamin A* as such is not found in plants but it is present in the form of carotenoids or pro-vitamins, usually accompanied by chlorophyll, although some plant materials such as carrots and maize contain carotenoids but no chlorophyll. The degree of greenness in hay and grass meals is therefore regarded as an indication of their carotene status. Carotenoids are readily converted by the horse into vitamin A, the change occurring in the intestinal wall and liver.

Weathering and overheating during storage destroys carotene. The carotene content of hay and grass meal is also reduced during normal storage by oxidation. Samples which are a year old should not be regarded as a satisfactory source of pro-vitamin A.

There are ten known forms of carotene — $\beta$ is the most active vitamin A precursor, followed by $\alpha$ while $\gamma$ has no vitamin A activity. Carotene has a very long chain in its molecule.

It can be split in the middle giving vitamin A from one or both halves, as vitamin A equals half the carotene molecule in most species. However, horses do not have the same conversion ratio and one I.U. of vitamin A is said to equal 0.4 mg of beta-carotene. The molecular

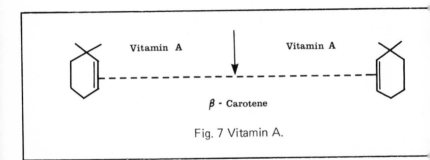

Fig. 7 Vitamin A.

rings can have subtle modifications and these decide whether or not they have vitamin A activity. For example, xanthophylls (oxygen-containing carotenoids), which are mainly responsible for the orange pigments in egg yolk, have no vitamin A activity.

Horses at grass store excess vitamin A in the liver and excess carotene in their body fat. After a normal season on good pasture, the accumulated storage is sufficient to satisfy the animal's requirements for about six months. After this the store will be depleted, unless the diet contains satisfactory levels of carotene. Broodmares in the last ninety days of gestation double their vitamin A requirement, so their supply will last only three months. The extra requirement for lactation depends on the mare's milk yield and is estimated to be 1.75 times the maintenance requirement[1], that for weaned foals and yearlings being 1.25 times maintenance. Unless broodmares have access to spring grass immediately after foaling, they must receive a dietary supply of the vitamin, since their store will have been utilised during gestation.

Vitamin A occurs naturally in fish liver oils; those of cod and halibut have long been used as important dietary supplements. It is also manufactured synthetically. The pure form is absorbed from the gut with greater efficiency than the carotenoids.

*The vitamin B-complex* is synthesised by gut microbes in the large intestine. Until foals develop a full complement of gut microbes, usually by the time they are seven months old, they have to rely on a dietary source of the vitamins. This is supplied by the mare's milk. Adult horses receiving antibiotic treatment may also require a dietary source of these vitamins.

Brewers' yeast is a rich source of B vitamins except for $B_{12}$. All are found in cereal grains and/or green leafy crops. Niacin is manufactured from the amino acid tryptophan, which is present in balanced rations. The production of $B_{12}$ is associated with a dietary supply of cobalt. Foals benefit from dietary supplementation of $B_{12}$

and brewers' yeast. Trials with adult stabled horses indicate that they may benefit from the administration of folic acid. $B_{12}$ and folic acid have been associated with curing anaemia and poor performance in racehorses.

*Vitamin C* is synthesised by horses, so there is normally no dietary requirement for this vitamin.

At least ten different forms of *vitamin D* are known. The two most important are ergocalciferol ($D_2$) and cholecalciferol ($D_3$). Both $D_2$ and $D_3$ are more stable to oxidation than vitamin A, $D_3$ being the most stable.

Vitamin D in plants is only found in sun-dried roughages and dead leaves. It occurs naturally in fish liver oils – halibut and cod liver oils are rich sources of $D_3$. The pro-vitamin (precursor) is present in the skin of animals but it has no vitamin value until it is converted into calciferols (sterol). For this to happen energy must be applied to the sterol molecule. This occurs when the horse's skin is subject to ultra-violet light from the sun. Activation is most effective with light wavelengths between $280-297$ nm$^2$, so the range is small. Clouds, smoke and dust particles affect radiation, the amount reaching the northern regions of the world in winter being slight. Ultra-violet light does not pass through glass, so that stabled horses, especially those exercised in the early morning, are likely to be deficient.

Vitamin D is essential for the proper absorption of calcium and phosphorus. High levels (fifty times the NRC 1978 recommendations of 6.6 I.U. per kilogramme of body weight per day) are considered to be harmful, and may result in soft tissue calcification, bone resorption and kidney damage.

The horse's requirement for *vitamin E* is not known. It has been used together with vitamin A and selenium to treat various conditions, notably to improve breeding performance in both mares and stallions and to prevent 'tying-up'. No success has been noted when it is used to prevent muscular degeneration and yellow fat disease in foals or to improve fertility in breeding stock, as mentioned above.

No studies have been made regarding *vitamin K* and its requirement by the horse. Vitamin E and vitamin K are both present in green herbage in adequate quantities to satisfy the demand of grazing horses. Cereal grains are usually fairly good sources of vitamin E, providing they are stored dry, without the addition of preservative acids (such as propcorn) or in a sealed bin. Vitamin K is synthesised by gut microbes in the large intestine.

Certain foodstuffs give a physiological response in excess of their food value. These contain unidentified factors which are thought to act in a similar way to vitamins. They include:

Spring grass                    Dried lucerne (alfalfa)
Fish meal                       Dried brewers' yeast
Dried whey

Vitamins can therefore be subdivided into the following categories:

Those for which the adult horse is said to have no dietary requirement except under stress conditions:

Vitamin C
Vitamin B-complex
Vitamin K

Those normally supplied by the diet in adequate amounts:

Vitamin E
Vitamin K
Vitamin B-complex

Vitamins subject to seasonal fluctuations:

Vitamin A
Vitamin D

Although a tremendous amount of information is available on vitamins, little work has been done on the horse's exact requirements. It is generally considered that increased metabolic demand is created for all nutrients by such factors as:

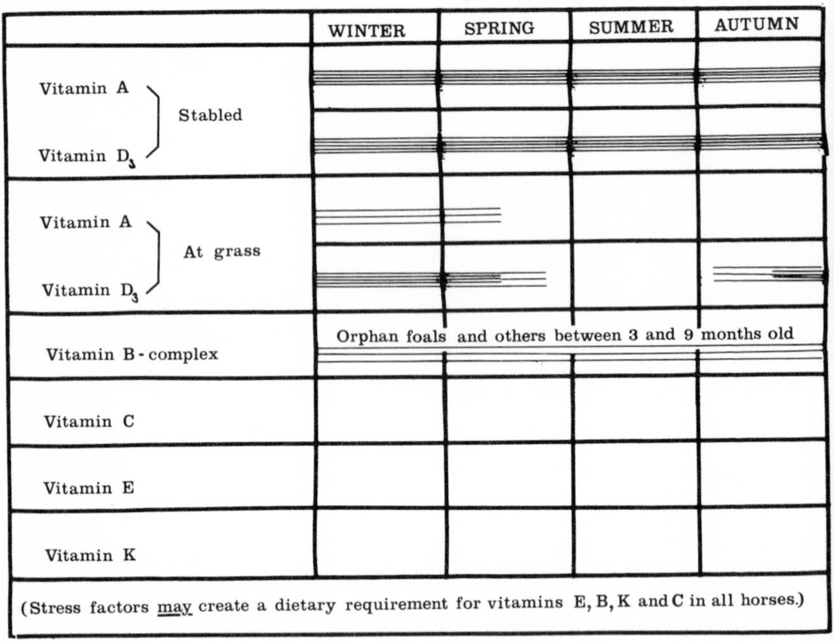

| | WINTER | SPRING | SUMMER | AUTUMN |
|---|---|---|---|---|
| Vitamin A ⎱ Stabled Vitamin D₃ ⎰ | ▬▬▬ | ▬▬▬ | ▬▬▬ | ▬▬▬ |
| | ▬▬▬ | ▬▬▬ | ▬▬▬ | ▬▬▬ |
| Vitamin A ⎱ At grass Vitamin D₃ ⎰ | ▬▬ | ▬▬ | | |
| | ▬▬ | ▬▬ | | ▬▬ |
| Vitamin B - complex | Orphan foals and others between 3 and 9 months old | | | |
| | ▬▬ | ▬▬ | ▬▬ | |
| Vitamin C | | | | |
| Vitamin E | | | | |
| Vitamin K | | | | |
| (Stress factors may create a dietary requirement for vitamins E, B, K and C in all horses.) | | | | |

Fig. 8 Vitamin requirements.

(1) *Stress*
Fast growth rates
The last ninety days of pregnancy
Lactation
Intense work
Travelling
Infection and ill health
Overcrowding and subclinical disease.
(2) *Environmental and seasonal conditions*
Horses stabled for long periods
Horses on low-quality forage diets
All horses during the winter months.
(3) *Genetic differences even within the same breed*
Certain individuals are more prone to nutritional deficiencies than others.

(4) *Nutrient inter-relationships*
   Rancidity destroys vitamin E
   Certain foodstuff preservatives are thought to destroy
   vitamin E
   A protein-like substance in raw egg white destroys
   biotin
   Some moulds in feed can increase requirements for
   particular vitamins, e.g. vitamin $D_3$.

Shortage of vitamins can have serious consequences.
Initially there are seldom any indications when horses
are getting inadequate supplies. The first sign is often a
general unthriftiness, which is difficult to diagnose until
more severe symptoms develop, when treatment can be
both difficult and expensive.

Single, uncomplicated, vitamin deficiencies do not
often occur in practice. It is relatively uncommon for a
diet to be so low in vitamins that marked deficiency
symptoms appear. However, borderline deficiencies can
represent an economic loss in terms of poor performance and reduced growth rates.

Access to well managed, leafy pasture and sunshine
minimises the need for supplementary vitamins in the
diet. Unfortunately, the paddock many horse owners
use as grazing is, in effect, little more than an exercise
yard, and sunlight is restricted in the northern hemi-
sphere. Stabled horses and those on poor grazing may
well need a vitamin supplement even during the summer
months.

It is mistaken kindness and a waste of money to use
vitamin preparations without regard to the type of
horse, its diet, and any stress factors involved. Horses in
high-risk categories should be given vitamin supplements
as a routine safeguard.

The following vitamin deficiency symptoms have
been noted in horses:
*Vitamin A*: poor growth, night blindness, excessive tear
gland secretion, keratinisation of the cornea and skin,

respiratory symptoms, abscess of the sublingual glands, reproductive problems and in extreme cases convulsive seizures and progressive weakness.

Prolonged feeding of excess vitamin A can cause bone fragility, hyperosteosis and exfoliated epithelium, but no danger is known to be associated with an excess of carotene.

*B-complex*:

Thiamin: loss of appetite and body weight, incoordination of muscles especially in the hind legs. Clinical examination shows lowered blood thiamin, elevated blood pyruvic acid and dilated and hypertrophied heart. Poisoning with bracken and yellow star thistle is due to a thiamin-destroying enzyme.

Vitamin $B_{12}$: no deficiency symptoms have been reported in horses but $B_{12}$ is associated with correcting anaemia in many species of animal. In humans a deficiency occurs in cases of pernicious anaemia.

Folic acid: malnourished stabled horses, showing poor performance and anaemia associated with low serum folic acid levels, have benefited from administration of this vitamin.

*Vitamin D*: a deficiency is characterised by reduced calcification of the bones, stiff and swollen joints and osteopetrosis (dense bones).

Excessive intakes of vitamin D lead to calcification of blood vessels, the heart and other soft tissue and bone abnormalities. Extensive bone deposits are found in ligaments, tendons and blood vessels.

High calcium intakes aggravate these effects.

*Vitamin E*: no clear evidence has been put forward to substantiate the claim that vitamin E improves breeding performance in horses. It has been used in conjunction with selenium to treat 'tying-up', but no evidence exists to confirm the value of vitamin E in curing this condition.

Many owners and trainers are well aware of the importance of vitamins in maintaining good health and performance in stock, and feed low levels of a wide-ranging supplement as a general precaution. However, because of the undesirable factors associated with excessively high vitamin intakes, veterinary advice should be sought before exceeding a supplier's recommendations for his product.

One would generally expect to find little need to feed a vitamin supplement to breeding stock and resting horses being summered on good-quality grass. However, mineral blocks are sometimes provided and these may be formulated to provide background levels of supplementary vitamins A and D.

REFERENCES

1 NRC *Nutrient Requirements of Horses* National Research Council, Washington D.C. **6**, 8-9, 16 (1978).
2 McDonald, P., Edwards, R.A. and Greenhalgh, J.F.D. *Animal Nutrition,* pub. Longman **5**, 66.

# 5 The Role of Minerals in Horse Feeding

Fifteen mineral elements are considered important in animal nutrition and these are known as the essential minerals. All must be present in the diet, since, unlike some vitamins, the horse is unable to manufacture his own supply. Their importance can be gauged from the fact that 3½-4½ per cent of the horse's total body weight is composed of mineral matter. Approximately 70 per cent of this is calcium and phosphorus. About 99 per cent of the body's calcium and 80 per cent of the phosphorus is found in bones and teeth. All essential elements function either structurally, electrochemically or catalytically; some − like magnesium − fulfil all three roles.

The following minerals are known to perform essential functions in the horse's body and therefore each must be present in the diet, within certain levels and proportions. They are normally divided into two groups, viz. major elements and trace elements according to requirement. Major elements are expressed in terms of percentage of the total diet, whereas trace elements are present in the body in concentrations no greater than 1 part/20,000 and are therefore expressed in terms of p.p.m. or mg./kg.

| *Major elements* | *Trace elements* |
|---|---|
| calcium | cobalt |
| phosphorus | iron |
| potassium | zinc |
| sodium | copper |
| chlorine | manganese |
| sulphur | iodine |
| magnesium | molybdenum |
| | selenium |

The elements can be further divided into:

(1) Those most deficient in rations:

calcium (in grass-based diets)

phosphorus (in lucerne [alfalfa] or other legume-based diets)

sodium

(2) Those most often associated with localised soil deficiencies or imbalances:

iodine

molybdenum

selenium

copper

calcium

(3) Those normally present in rations at satisfactory levels:

| | |
|---|---|
| potassium | cobalt |
| sulphur | iron |
| magnesium | zinc |
| manganese | iodine |

The number and level of minerals added to a ration is determined by the following factors:

(1) Stress conditions, such as work, lactation and growth.

(2) Minerals naturally present in the diet. These in turn are related to:

(a) type of grain and roughage fed;

(b) mineral status and pH of soil in which the plants were grown;

(c) D-value of the forage (see below);

(d) grass species present in hay or the sward;

(e) legume content of the hay or sward;

(f) maturity of the grazed sward and season of the year.

(g) herbal content of the sward or inclusion of a herbal strip.

Plants vary in their ability to take up individual minerals from the soil. For instance, legumes such as clover or lucerne and root crops contain more calcium than grain. Herbs can increase the availability of minerals in pasture and hay due to their deeper root systems and slower growth rates.

As plants age, the percentage of water, protein and most minerals declines and the percentage of fibre and calcium increases. D-value is a measure of the percentage of digestible organic matter in the dry matter of feed and therefore reflects the relationship between the maturity and the food value of forage. Mature grass hay is likely to be deficient in available calcium and phosphorus.

Horses may consume some soil while grazing but otherwise their entire mineral needs are naturally supplied from those taken up by plants during growth. Those present are directly related to the mineral status of the soil, which is affected by: geological area; climate; fertiliser treatment; type of stock carried by grassland; management of the sward.

Horses at grass depend on herbage for their essential minerals. Calcium is particularly important for youngstock and lactating mares. On poor, acid soils, stock may not obtain sufficient calcium from the herbage and bone disorders can result. Acid soils (pH 5.5-6.0) result in the disappearance of better grasses and clover and their replacement with poor wiry unpalatable species having a lower food value. The optimum soil pH for grassland is considered to be 6.5. Over-liming can lead to lower levels of certain minerals, such as manganese, being taken up by the plants, or an increased uptake of certain undesirable trace elements in some areas, such as molybdenum which impairs copper metabolism in cattle and horses.

Natural limestone and chalk areas have long been considered desirable for horse breeding.

Rainwater in industrial areas, or in the path of the prevailing wind blowing across industrial areas, may contain sulphur dioxide. This forms weak solutions of sulphurous acid, creating acid conditions in the top soil, and a build-up of soil sulphur which, if not corrected, may lead to mineral deficiencies in grazing stock. This can be a problem, especially in districts where there is a high rainfall.

Trace element deficiencies are usually associated with particular soils but they can be induced in *any* area by indiscriminate use of lime and fertilisers.

Minerals are recycled by the animal's body to a variable extent but a percentage of each is lost in the faeces, urine and through the skin; some are therefore returned to the land by grazing stock. The *net require- ment* for minerals is expressed as the sum of the animal's maintenance requirement plus the requirement for growth, lactation or pregnancy. This is supplied by plant material and/or mineral supplements. Animals with the highest net requirement remove the most mine- rals from land, so young fast-growing cattle or milking cows should not be grazed on land used to rear young horses, as they will compete for the available minerals. Mature cattle with a maintenance-only requirement are preferred.

Efficient grassland management entails presenting stock with adequate palatable grass throughout the graz- ing season. Rotational grazing at three- or four-week intervals and regular topping where necessary ensures a continuing even growth of 'young' herbage and prevents the fall in nutritional value associated with grass which has been allowed to go to seed.

The stem and leaves of plants vary significantly in mineral content. Leaves contain more calcium, mag- nesium, sulphur and iron than stems and older tissue. Since horses are, by nature, very selective grazers, care- ful paddock management is essential to maintain maxi- mum nutritional value.

Legumes, such as clover, contain higher levels than grass of calcium, cobalt, magnesium, molybdenum, iron, manganese, copper, boron, as well as nitrogen. Some species of grass contain more minerals than others but the difference is slight as compared with that between grasses and legumes. Most broad-leaved 'herbs' are rich in minerals.

*Calcium* and *phosphorus* are the two most important minerals in terms of quantities required; they are always considered together. They are essential for the production of normal structure and function of bone. Both minerals are also essential as co-factors in many of the complex chemical reactions of the body's metabolism. Phosphorus is absorbed from the colon and calcium from the small intestine.

When designing rations for horses, care must be taken to assess the quantity of calcium and phosphorus present in the available foods and to correct any deficiency. Retention of calcium by the body depends largely on the presence of phosphorus and vitamin D. A deficiency of either calcium or phosphorus causes bone disease, whereas an excess of either tends to 'lock up' the other by forming insoluble salts and so increasing the deficiency. An unusually wide ratio between these elements can affect utilisation of certain trace elements. It is therefore advisable to establish the optimum phosphorus requirement before adjusting the calcium:phosphorus ratio.

The following figures should be used as a basis for calculations[1]:

|  | On DM (dry matter) basis |
|---|---|
| Foals (3 months old) | . . . . . 0.60% phosphorus |
| Weaned foals | . . . . . 0.50% phosphorus |
| Yearlings | . . . . . 0.40% phosphorus |
| Pregnant mares | . . . . . 0.35% phosphorus |
| Lactating mares | . . . . . 0.35% phosphorus |
| Adults (maintenance) | . . . . . 0.20% phosphorus |
| Light exercise | . . . . . 0.20% phosphorus |

The following calcium:phosphorus ratios are considered by the author to be satisfactory and allow a small margin of safety for variations in availability:

|                  | On DM (dry matter) basis |
|------------------|--------------------------|
| Foals            | . . . . . . . . . . . . . . 1.5:1 |
| Yearlings        | . . . . . . . . . . . . . . 1.7:1 |
| Mature horses    | . . . . . . . . . . . . . . 2.0:1 |
| Pregnant mares   | . . . . . . . . . . . . . . 3.0:1 |
| Lactating mares  | . . . . . . . . . . . . . . 3.0:1 |
| Light work       | . . . . . . . . . . . . . . 2.0:1 |

Work does *not* affect the ratio.

The calcium:phosphorus levels of a diet may be calculated as follows:

Multiply the percentage of phosphorus and calcium in each food by the percentage of that food in the ration. Add up the total of each column, divide by 100 to give the percentage of calcium and phosphorus in the mix. Adjust the phosphorus figure if necessary by the addition of a supplement containing phosphorus. Work out the calcium:phosphorus ratio and adjust this to optimum requirement by the addition of a calcium supplement.

The availability of calcium and phosphorus in feeds and additives is variable. Riechel (1970) reported that conventional supplements are relatively unavailable to the horse[2]. However, Hintz and Schryver (1976) give the following availability figures[3]:

| Beet pulp           | 60% of the calcium |
|---------------------|--------------------|
| Flaked maize        | 32% of the phosphorus |
| Milk products       | 79% of the calcium and 64% of the phosphorus |
| Oats                | 40% of the phosphorus |
| Bran                | 29% of the phosphorus |
| Lucerne hay         | 77% of the calcium and 44% of the phosphorus |
| Bone meal           | 71% of the calcium and 58% of the phosphorus |
| Dicalcium phosphate | 74% of the calcium and 58% of the phosphorus |
| Limestone           | 69% of the calcium |

When working out calcium:phosphorus ratios it is therefore important to bear the availability factor in mind. The following supplements are commonly used to balance rations for horses:

|  | % phosphorus | % calcium |
|---|---|---|
| Ground limestone (calcium carbonate) | – | 38.0 |
| Dicalcium phosphate | 17.9 | 23.6 |
| Calcium lactate | – | 13.0 |
| Calcium gluconate | – | 9.0 |
| Bone meal (steamed bone flour) | 13.5 | 38.5 |

As well as conferring rigidity and shape on the horse's body, bones act as reservoirs for calcium and phosphorus. At times of negative mineral balance, for instance during the first half of lactation or when an unbalanced diet is fed over a long period, large amounts of these minerals are released from bone. This process is controlled by the parathyroid hormones, calcitonin and thyroxine, which are responsible for the regulation of blood calcium.

Inadequate levels of dietary calcium or phosphorus may result in decreased bone strength, resulting in crooked legs and enlarged joints in foals or weakened bones and obscure lameness in mature animals.

Calcium has been fed at levels over five times the requirement with no ill effects providing phosphorus is adequate to compensate for reduced absorption. Excess phosphorus coupled with low levels of calcium, for instance diets containing high levels of bran, result in nutritional secondary hyperparathyroidism, leading to osteofibrosis (bran disease or big head). This causes enlargement of the jaw and face, also obscure lameness and splints. This is due to removal of calcium from the outer areas of bone to help rectify the blood ratio. The ligament attachments are loosened and may tear since they are now attached to fibrous tissue rather than

 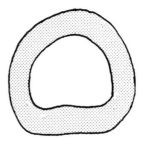

Note the thickness and strength of the normal bone on the right as compared with that of a deficient horse on the left.

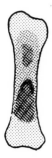 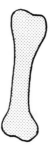

Diagrams representing X-ray photographs of bones from a deficient horse on the left and normal horse on the right. The size of bone is not necessarily an indication of it s strength since nature often thickens bone to help counteract a structural weakness.

Fig. 9 Effect of calcium, phosphorus or vitamin D deficiency on bone.

bone[4]. This is one cause of splints, due to tearing away of the interosseous ligament between the splint bone and cannon bone[5]. Phosphorus deficiency is associated with infertility in other species.

Assessment of the horse's calcium and phosphorus status by means of blood and hair analysis has not proved successful. Accurately balanced rations to ensure correct levels in the diet are therefore essential to avoid deficiency symptoms.

*Potassium* is concerned with osmotic regulation of body fluids, nerve and muscle excitability and also carbohydrate metabolism. The potassium content of plants is very high – most forages contain in excess of 1.5 per cent potassium, which is more than animals need. It is therefore very unlikely that horses at grass or those receiving adequate supplies of hay will suffer from a deficiency. Dietary excess is excreted in the urine but very high intakes are thought to interfere with magnesium absorption.

Potassium needs for young foals are given as 206-288 mg./kg. body wt./day[6]. For adult horses 60 mg./kg. body wt./day is recommended[7]. Deficiency symptoms include decreased growth rate and reduced appetite.

*Sodium* and *chlorine* are, like potassium, mainly concerned with acid-base balance and osmotic regulation of body fluids. Most sodium is ingested in the form of sodium chloride (common salt) and most is excreted in this form as sweat. Prolonged exercise, hard work and hot weather increase requirement. The horse's exact requirement is unknown, but if salt is offered free choice a deficiency is unlikely to occur.

Where deficiencies do occur it is thought that sodium rather than chlorine is the limiting factor. Some other minerals are usually present as chlorides. No symptoms have been recorded in horses, but in other species they include depraved appetite, rough coat, reduced growth rates and lowered milk production. Excessive amounts of salt increase thirst and cause digestive disturbances.

Since *sulphur* is an integral part of the amino acids methionine and cystine, horses fed balanced diets containing high-quality protein do not suffer from a deficiency of this mineral.

Rainwater in industrial areas may contain high levels of sulphur which can interfere with the uptake of certain trace elements, notably copper.

Horses are not affected by *magnesium* deficiency to the same extent as cattle. Their requirement is based on the relationship between retention and intake; for adults this is given as 1.3 g./100 kg. body wt. and for youngstock as 12-18 mg./kg. body wt. per day[8].

The trace elements *iron, manganese, molybdenum* and *cobalt* have not been specifically studied in relation to the horse. There have been comparative studies on the concentration in the tissues of equines and ruminants as well as a general review of the value of multivitamin/mineral supplements for the well-being of horses. However, none have led to any specific recommendations. It is suggested that horses heavily infected with worms may suffer from iron deficiency and anaemia. Cobalt is an integral part of the vitamin $B_{12}$ molecule.

*Zinc* deficiency can be induced in foals by feeding zinc deficient diets, but normal diets will contain enough to satisfy the animal's needs. A diet containing 40 p.p.m. appears adequate[9]. Toxicity levels seem to be very high probably in excess of 1,000 p.p.m. Deficiency symptoms noted include reduced growth rates, alopecia and cutaneous lesions on the lower legs.

There is an apparent relationship between low serum *copper* levels and haemorrhages in older foaling mares. This suggests either reduced ability to absorb or to mobilise copper stores with advancing age.

Molybdenum levels of 5 to 25 p.p.m. interfere with copper utilisation[10]. Molybdenum-induced copper deficiency has been implicated as a cause of 'rickets-like' disease in foals in Ireland. Unsuitable levels of dietary sulphur also interfere with copper utilisation; this can be a problem in industrial areas.

Work with pregnant pony mares revealed that no adverse effects resulted, to either the mares or their foals, when intakes of copper as high as 791 mg./kg. of food for 183 days were given[11].

Copper deficiency occurs in cattle in certain areas. Affected animals fail to thrive. Depigmentation of the coat, especially round the eye, is a characteristic feature. Similar symptoms of depigmentation in horses respond to broad-spectrum mineral supplementation.

The requirement for *iodine* is 0.10 mg./day. Excess iodine in pregnant mares has been shown to cause toxicity and goitre in foals. Care should therefore be taken when feeding seaweed meals (kelp) because of its high iodine content.

*Selenium* is an integral part of an erythrocyte (blood cell) enzyme. In certain areas of the world selenium reaches a level as high as 5-40 p.p.m. in natural foodstuffs. This results in the development of 'alkali disease' symptoms, such as loss of hair from the mane and tail and rings on the hooves. Requirement is estimated to be 240 mg./100 kg. body wt. per day[12]. Selenium requirement is related to vitamin E content of the diet; diets low in vitamin E give a higher dietary selenium requirement. High dietary sulphur levels can interfere with the utilisation of selenium. UK herbage normally contains between 0.06 and 0.15 mg./kg. DM of selenium.

The optimum dietary level for major elements depends on the digestibility of forage and the class of animal being fed. The mineral demands of pregnant, lactating mares and youngstock are significantly higher than those of other horses. Requirements of horses for trace elements cannot be stated with precision, so it is only possible to indicate levels currently considered desirable. The 'satisfactory' level for a particular element can be influenced by the concentration of other elements present in the ration. For instance, given the right

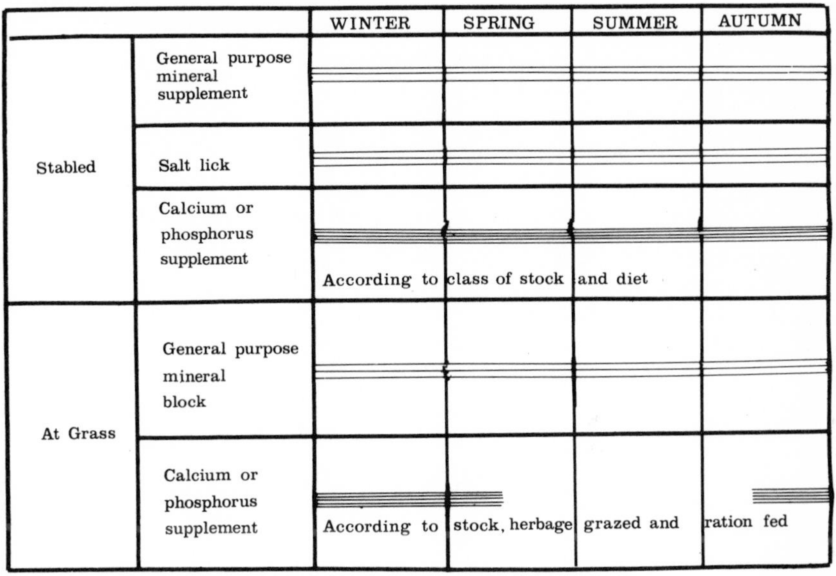

| | | WINTER | SPRING | SUMMER | AUTUMN |
|---|---|---|---|---|---|
| Stabled | General purpose mineral supplement | | | | |
| | Salt lick | | | | |
| | Calcium or phosphorus supplement | According to | class of stock | and diet | |
| At Grass | General purpose mineral block | | | | |
| | Calcium or phosphorus supplement | According to | stock, herbage | grazed and | ration fed |

Fig. 10 Mineral requirements.

circumstances a three-way 'interaction' may be produced of which copper-molybdenum-sulphur is the best known. Others include: calcium-phosphorus-magnesium; sodium-potassium; potassium-magnesium; calcium-zinc-copper-iron-manganese-iodine; copper-zinc-iron; copper-iodine. Therefore, unless a specific mineral deficiency has been diagnosed it is unwise to add elements other than calcium, phosphorus or salt to a ration. This practice could trigger off a deficiency chain reaction. Most trainers and stud managers use wide-ranging mineral supplements to safeguard the health of their horses. In hot weather there is an increased loss of body fluids and electrolytes so many endurance riders administer low levels of electrolytes in their horse's feed or water.

REFERENCES
1   NRC *Nutrient Requirements of Horses* National

Research Council, Washington, D.C. **6**, 6-8 (1978).

2 Reichel, E.C. Letter to the editor *J. Am. Vet. Med. Asscn.* **156**, 524-5 (1970).

3 Hintz, H.F. and Schryver, H.F. 'Nutrition and Bone Development in Horses' *J. Am. Vet. Med. Asscn.* **168**, 1, 39-44 (1976).

4 Brook, D. 'Osteoporosis in a six year old pony' *Equine Vet. J.* **7**, 46-8 (1975).

5 Rooney, J.R. *The Lame Horse*, pub. A.S. Barnes & Co. 2, 67-8 (1977).

6 Stowe, H.D. 'Effects of potassium in a purified equine diet' *J. Nutr.* **101**, 629 (1971).

7 Hintz, H.F. and Schryver, H.F. 'Potassium metabolism in ponies' *J. Anim. Sci.* **42**, 637 (1976).

8 Schryver *et al.* 'Mineral composition of the whole body, liver and bone of young horses' *J. Nutr.* **104**, 126 (1974).

9 Tyznik, W.J. 'Recent advances in horse nutrition' Ohio State Univ. (1978).

10 Walsh, J. and O'Moore, L.B. 'Excess of Molybdenum in Herbage as a Possible Contributory Factor in Equine Osteodystrophia' *Nature* **171**, 1166 (1953).

11 Smith *et al.* 'Tolerance of ponies to high levels of dietary copper' *J. Anim. Sci.* **41**, 1645 (1975).

12 Stowe, H.D. 'Serum selenium and related parameters of naturally and experimentally fed horses' *J. Nutr.* **93**, 60 (1967).

# 6 Nutrient Requirements of the Adult Horse

The human factor plays as large a part as any other in feeding horses. The horse has to rely on us for most of, if not all his needs. Some people are naturally good feeders, but many tend to overfeed their animals, and this is probably the most common fault of all. These people really enjoy feeding horses. Mostly their animals are under-exercised but still fed as though they were in hard work. Consequently they become fatter and fatter. Their owners are delighted with the response they get to high-energy rations and appear to derive pleasure from watching over-fat animals waddling contentedly round the paddocks. Overfeeding is costly and can be detrimental to the horse's health, performance and lifespan, so it is definitely not recommended. Some show and sale animals are deliberately overfed to satisfy the judge and buyers.

Other people tend to over-horse themselves. They are frightened to feed their animals well, as they imagine they will never be able to control them. This, too, is bad for the horse.

A very few people are just too mean to spend money on food.

The good feeder recognises the link between nutrition, health and performance. Many suggestions for diets and additions to diets, supposed to help increase performance, have been put forward over the years. These have been mainly based on tradition, or the whims and experience of owners, trainers and grooms. Since nutrition has developed as a science it has been possible to investigate many of these claims and in some cases refute their use as aids to better feeding and performance. Some may work, however, when a horse is well fed. Any resul-

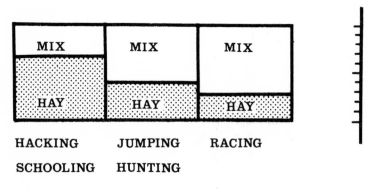

Fig. 11 The energy density of the ration is increased with work. This automatically increases the percentage protein and so takes care of the protein requirement which is a constant proportion of the energy requirement.

ting increment due entirely to nutrition is likely to be small, but even a small increase could make all the difference between winning or losing an important race or competition.

Adult horses must be given rations which balance energy intake with requirement: this is commonly expressed in terms of digestible energy (DE). Other systems (e.g. metabolisable energy or net energy) may be more accurate but information is not available for the horse.

The horse's nutritional requirement for energy is met by glucose, fatty acids and surplus protein. A horse on a normal diet of hay and oats will derive most of its glucose from the hydrolysis of starch in grain. This takes place in, and is absorbed from, the small intestine, whereas the fatty acids are synthesised by gut microbes in the large intestine, as an end product to the breakdown of fibre. Glucose is considered by many to be the better source of energy for muscle metabolism[1].

Horses have a flexible metabolism pattern: on high-grain diets they adopt a pattern similar to monogastric animals, on high-fibre diets closer to ruminants.

The horse depends on bacteria in the large intestine to break down fibre. Certain bacteria are specific to certain types of food, so when dietary changes are made it takes time for the bacterial population to adjust. Until the appropriate bacteria have become sufficiently numerous they will not be able to digest the new foodstuff efficiently. In general, the more dissimilar the feeds the lower digestive efficiency becomes. Maximum efficiency is obtained by keeping to the same rations each day and by feeding smaller amounts more often, i.e. by dividing the total ration up into three to four feeds and offering hay ad lib. as far as possible. Any system which leads to greater consistency of material in the large intestine is desirable.

Common foodstuffs high in starch energy include oats, barley and maize.

Common foodstuffs high in fibre energy include hay, dried sugar beet pulp, bran, dried grass and lucerne.

Cooking is thought to increase digestible energy of grain by 3 per cent as it ruptures the starch granules increasing the efficiency of enzyme action in the small intestine. Some foods — for example, sugar beet pulp — contain a more highly digestible fibre than others. The percentage of digestible organic matter in the dry matter of roughage is as follows:

| | |
|---|---|
| Carrots | 81 |
| Sugar beet pulp | 79 |
| Dried grass | 70 |
| Bran | 61 |
| Dried lucerne | 60 |
| Grass hay | 60 |
| Clover hay | 57 |
| Lucerne hay | 55 |
| Barley straw | 49 |
| Oat straw | 46 |

Chopping or milling increases rate of passage through

the digestive tract by 14 per cent when compared with loose hay, and therefore affects intake; pelleting increases intake by 21 per cent[2]. Adult horses consume approximately 2.5 per cent of their body weight in food per day. This limited capacity for food can be used to advantage when controlling energy intake and must be considered when feeding horses with a high energy requirement.

In any given situation a horse has a particular DE requirement and a particular dry matter intake. Therefore, for all horses but most particularly those in work, each kg. of the ration must contain the number of megajoules (MJ) of DE to satisfy demand, otherwise weight loss will take place. A horse in hard work needs a high-grain, low-roughage diet. Good-quality hay alone will satisfy the maintenance requirement of adult horses, but poor-quality hay has a very low digestible energy value. A horse fed the correct weight of this diet alone each day would not receive enough energy to keep himself alive and so would decline rapidly into starving condition. High-fibre hay of low digestibility is broken down more slowly by the gut microbes and this tends to limit appetite and cause 'pot-bellies'.

The diagram opposite shows the adult horse's requirement for energy in relation to liveweight and work. Many factors affect the energy requirement including: training, weight and ability of the rider and environment.

The megajoules (MJ) of digestible energy in excess of maintenance required for strenuous effort are approximately 78 times those required for walking exercise.

The heavier the horse the greater the amount of extra dietary energy required to perform a given amount of work. This may be a valid point to bear in mind when selecting animals for riding schools and trekking centres.

The adequacy of a ration in relation to its energy should be judged by observing the animal's body condition by regular scoring and adjusting the diet accordingly. Individual horses differ greatly in the amount of

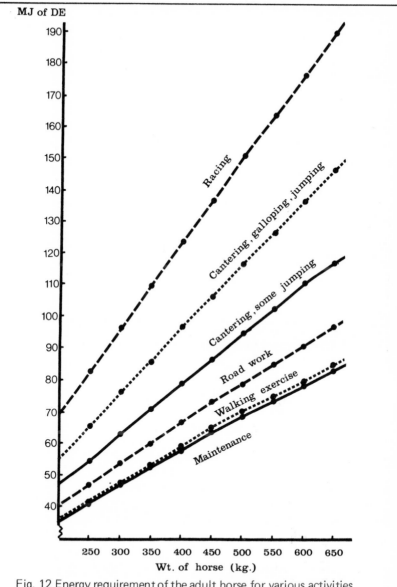

Fig. 12 Energy requirement of the adult horse for various activities according to body weight. (By kind permission of the NRC[3].)

energy they use – even animals of the same breed and size, performing the same work. A cursory visual assessment of condition can be surprisingly inaccurate, so most leading trainers weigh their horses regularly. By obtaining a weight record it is possible to tell how each horse is responding to its diet and work.

Horses have an individual optimum or racing weight which coincides with peak fitness and performance. Where animals are to race or compete extensively throughout a long season, it is vital that once their optimum weight has been established any weight lost should be regained before the next outing, so that peak performance can be maintained throughout the season. This system affords maximum economy as it also reduces the incidence of over or under feeding.

The horse's absolute weight is not the major factor, as each will have an optimum weight according to its size, age, conformation and fitness. Weight change either side of optimum is important – this is the 'barometer' for all feeding and training programmes.

Weighing or measuring should take place at the start of training and be repeated at monthly intervals. When the horse competes he should be weighed or measured immediately before and after the race or competition and then weekly until optimum weight has been regained. A survey involving eight Thoroughbred horses in training indicated that average weight loss per race was −7.3 kg. with the greatest loss occurring after the first outing of the season: average −12.6 kg. as compared with only −3.5 kg. subsequently. Weighing was used as a means of pin pointing the racing weight of each horse, commensurate with peak performance. For example:

| Body wt. when raced | | Result |
|---|---|---|
| kg. | (lb.) | |
| 489.9 | (1,080) | unplaced |
| 469.0 | (1,034) | placed 3rd |
| 465.4 | (1,026) | unplaced |
| 469.9 | (1,036) | won |

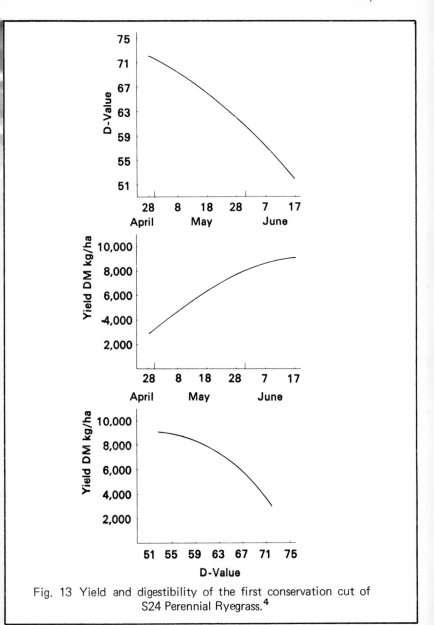

Fig. 13 Yield and digestibility of the first conservation cut of S24 Perennial Ryegrass.[4]

Good-quality hay is the key to feeding all horses. Eighty per cent of the nutrients are contained in the leaf. The older the grass is allowed to become before cutting, the greater the yield but the less digestible it is and therefore the lower its nutritional value.

Digestibility is measured in terms of D-value. This is the percentage of digestible organic matter in the total dry matter. The National Institute of Agricultural Botany (NIAB) recommends 67D as being the optimum level of quality commensurate with a reasonable hay crop[4]. Any further increase in yield is normally accompanied by a rapid decline in digestibility. The decision when to cut is a complex one involving such additional factors as cleanliness of the crop. Hay usually has a slightly lower D-value than the standing crop. Barn-drying results in the least loss, whereas weathered hay has the greatest; the range is normally 1-10 digestibility units. In Fig. 13 mid-May is shown as the date for Early Perennial Ryegrass but this may be ten days or so later in the North of England. Drought conditions would result in a premature decline in digestibility.

At the recommended time of cutting, grass is frequently deficient in protein. Italian ryegrass may contain only 6.6 per cent of the dry matter at 67 D and perennial ryegrass 8.2 per cent. Low protein is often associated with high yield. In second crop hay the yield is lower, more soil nitrogen is therefore available per unit of dry matter, so the protein content tends to be higher but energy is lower. The relationship between D-value, DE (digestible energy), CP (crude protein) and performance is clearly demonstrated by comparing Figs. 14 and 23. Stud A used hay sample A, stud B, hay B, and stud C, hay C.

Ideally, hay bought in bulk for use in stables should be analysed before purchase. Without knowledge of its quality a feeding programme is merely guesswork. A representative sample from each batch should be placed in a polythene fridge bag, clearly labelled and sent to a laboratory for testing. Most large manufacturers of compound horse foods will carry out the analysis for you free of charge if you use their products, otherwise samples should be sent to an ADAS nutritional chemistry laboratory. It usually takes two weeks before the results come back.

A rough estimate of the quality of a bale can be made by examining its colour and smell − a good sample should appear green and smell sweet, with no sign of mould. Take a section from the middle of the bale, one foot (30 cm.) long, hold it like a concertina, bang it down onto a sheet of plastic spread over a hard floor and examine what falls out.

A lot of loose leaf = good hay.

A lot of seeds = very mature hay.

Fig. 14 below shows the analysis of three typical 'horse' hays.

In order to avoid dust and mould spores, many horse owners select mature hays, with a lot of stem and little leaf. Most years it is possible to buy good, leafy hay which is also clean. Good-quality hay, 8.5 per cent crude protein (CP) or over, will supply the maintenance requirements of all adult horses and ponies. The lower the value of the hay the more concentrates will be needed to balance the ration. Buying good hay is therefore sound economic practice.

| | | On DM basis | | |
|---|---|---|---|---|
| | | Per cent crude protein | MJ DE/kg | D-value |
| A | 50:50 Lucerne/Grass | 9·9 | 8·1 | 53·9 |
| B | Grass | 5·2 | 7·3 | 48·3 |
| C | Grass | 3·9 | 8·8 | 57·3 |

Fig. 14 Comparison of three 'horse' hays.

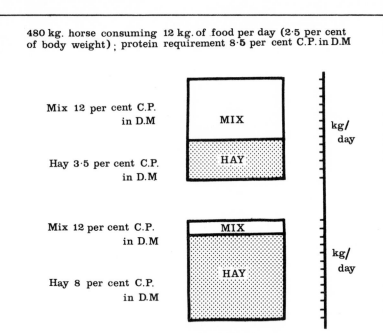

480 kg. horse consuming 12 kg. of food per day (2·5 per cent of body weight); protein requirement 8·5 per cent C.P. in D.M

Mix 12 per cent C.P. in D.M

Hay 3·5 per cent C.P. in D.M

kg/ day

Mix 12 per cent C.P. in D.M

Hay 8 per cent C.P. in D.M

kg/ day

Fig. 15 The wisdom of feeding good hay.

Mature horses require 8.5 per cent CP in their diet[3]. Work does not increase the percentage requirement, but since a higher energy demand is met by feeding more concentrates and less hay, this will also take care of any increase in demand for protein. Horses should receive at least 0.6 kg. of hay per 100 kg. body weight[5]. For a 450 kg. horse this amounts to 2.7 kg. (6 lb.) per day. However the quantity normally given to horses in training is in the region of 10-15 lb. (4.5-6.8 kg.) per day.

Adult horses do not have a critical requirement for amino acids — that is, they are indifferent to protein quality. Microbial protein synthesis in the caecum and colon improves the biological value of dietary protein and compensates for any shortfall in the ration. It is not known how efficient microbial protein absorption is, so it is considered safer to supplement the diet of animals under stress with a source of high-grade protein. However care should be taken when feeding horses in fast work, since excess protein is used as a source of energy and may be laid down as fat. When a high level of dietary protein is fed to working horses it can be detrimental to optimum performance, as it increases heart and respiration rates and sweating[6]. However the inclusion of 2.5 per cent extracted soyabean meal in a ration based on oats should be safe for animals in hard work.

An 8.5 per cent CP hay will, in most cases, supply enough dietary energy for animals in slow work. Any deficiency in protein or energy is made good by means of a concentrate mix. The source of energy for the mix will depend largely on the type of horse being fed and work performed. A horse or pony which is to remain quiet to ride but needs additional protein and energy should receive this from the intermediate foodstuffs (see Appendix 1, page 102). Animals in fast work should be given a concentrate ration based on oats. Those in thin condition, or losing weight, may be offered high-energy grain such as cracked maize as part of their diet, in most cases not exceeding 5 per cent of the ration. An even greater weight gain can be achieved by cooking grain, e.g. boiled oats for horses in fast work and boiled barley or flaked maize for horses in slow work.

Recommended maximum daily quantities of foodstuffs in a ration (all data percentage fresh weight basis):

| | |
|---|---|
| Oats | 90 |
| Barley | 25 |
| Maize | 30 |
| Linseed | 10 |
| Bran | 10 |
| Dried sugar beet pulp | 10 |
| Fish meal | 10 |
| Extracted soyabean meal | 15 |
| Dried yeast | 5 |

Horses and ponies at grass should be weighed monthly or their weight estimated. Weight change is then related to optimum condition and this in turn linked to the nutritional value and quantity of herbage available, with additional food offered only when necessary. While grass is the natural food for horses, it is not a balanced diet at all times of the year. Young leafy grass, for example, has an excess of protein and high water content which may restrict intake of nutrients. However, it also contains unidentified factors which give a metabolic response out of all proportion to nutritional value. Water content of herbage varies throughout the year from 90 per cent in early season to 50 per cent when the plants have seeded. The structural tissues are largely cellulose and fibre. The remainder of the plant consists of cell contents made up from sugars, lipids, proteins, organic acids, minerals, vitamins and other substances. Carbohydrates are the most abundant.

The amount of cellulose increases as the plant matures. Pure cellulose is broken down by the gut microbes but its digestibility is reduced according to the amount of lignin present, which increases with age. Paddocks should therefore be topped regularly throughout the season to ensure a continuing supply of 'young' herbage, and therefore maximum nutritional value.

Muscle glycogen and free fatty acids play a major role in supplying energy to the muscles of fit and unfit horses[7]. A fit horse can adapt to use both fat and glycogen to meet an increased energy demand. The unfit horse cannot oxidise or use fat as efficiently as the fit horse but instead uses more muscle glycogen.

No data are available on the benefits of adding fat to horse diets but studies involving other species have shown improved performance.

The addition of fat raises the energy level of the diet and therefore increases the protein requirement. Vitamin E supplements would be beneficial with unsaturated vegetable oils. Heat treated, full fat soyabean meal may be used in rations to replace extracted soya-bean meal.

## REFERENCES

1 Argenzia, J.B. and Hintz, H.F. 'Glucose tolerance and the effect of volatile fatty acid on plasma glucose concentration in ponies' *J. Anim. Sci.* **30**, 514 (1970).
2 Haenlein, C.F.W. *et al.* 'Comparative response of horses and sheep to different physical forms of alfalfa hay' *J. Anim. Sci.* **25**, 740 (1966).
3 NRC *Nutrient Requirements of Horses* National Research Council, Washington, D.C. **6**, 2, 21 (1978).
4 NIAB *Grasses and Legumes for Conservation 1979/80* Technical Leaflet No. 2, National Institute of Agricultural Botany, Cambridge.
5 Olsson, N. and Ruudvere, A. 'The Nutrition of the Horse' *Nutr. Abst. Rev.* **25**, 1 (1955).
6 Slade, **L.M.** *et al.* '**Nutritional Adaptions** of Horses for End**urance Perf**ormance' in *Proceedings of the Fourth Equine Nutrition Symposium* Calif. State Polytech. Univ., Pomona (1975).
7 Goodman, H.M., Vander Noot, G.W., Trout, J.R. and Squibb, R.L. *J. Anim Sci.* **37**, 1 (1973).

# 7 Nutrient Requirements of the Broodmare

Most breeders aim to produce a strong, viable foal from their mares each year. For this, good nutrition is essential. Over-fat mares (condition score 4 to 5) are notoriously difficult to get in foal – excess weight appears to have a depressant effect on the pituitary gland or correct hormonal status of the animal. Over-fat, under-exercised, in-foal mares may have difficulty foaling. Under-nourished mares (condition score 0 to 1) may have smaller foals (see Fig. 19) and reduced udder development, while barren and maiden mares in this condition usually remain in anoestrus until the weather is warmer and the spring grass grows. Poor feeding and excessive weight loss after foaling can, among other things, reduce milk yield and so in turn affect the foal.

There is little information available on the energy requirement for pregnancy. The NRC (1978) recommendations suggest that since the foetus grows fastest during the last ninety days of gestation the added requirement is calculated entirely for this period[1]. Therefore for the first eight months of pregnancy the mare should be fed exactly the same way as any other adult horse. In-foal mares may be ridden as usual for the first three months of pregnancy. Some Thoroughbred fillies remain in training and race on the flat during this period. Their diet is then identical to other horses in work or training. Quiet hacking exercise can be continued until the mare becomes too heavy to ride.

For broodmares not in work or lactating, maintenance levels of energy and protein are considered satisfactory for conception and development of the foetus. During early pregnancy, foetal growth rate is extremely low and protein utilisation by the mare enhanced, there-

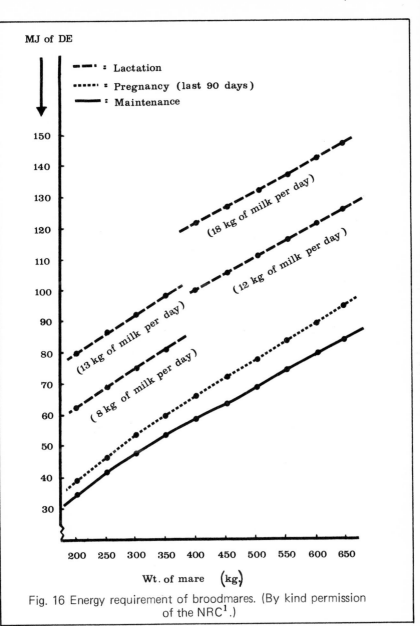

Fig. 16 Energy requirement of broodmares. (By kind permission of the NRC[1].)

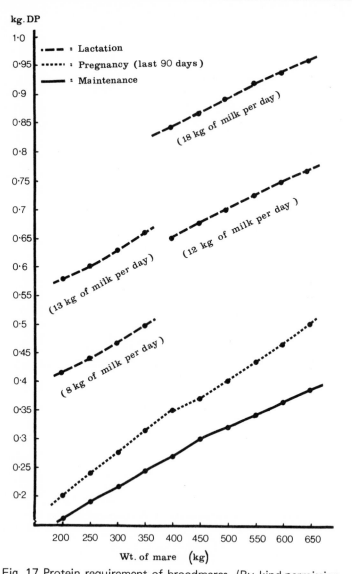

Fig. 17 Protein requirement of broodmares. (By kind permission of the NRC[1].)

fore a maintenance ration is considered satisfactory. In a group of ten lactating mares at grass day and night but affected by drought conditions at about 120 days post partum, it was found that the one barren mare lost weight at the rate of −1.1 kg./day, as compared with an average of −0.4 kg./day for the rest of the group. During the last ninety days of pregnancy there is a rapid increase in demand for all nutrients.

The pregnancy requirement for energy is estimated to be 12 per cent higher than maintenance[1]. Energy intakes in excess of 6 per cent over maintenance result in lower weight losses after foaling[2,3]. Fig. 18 shows the average liveweight change before and after foaling of thirty-six Thoroughbred mares on three different studs.

The voluntary intake of food decreases as the developing foetus increases in size, so there must be a

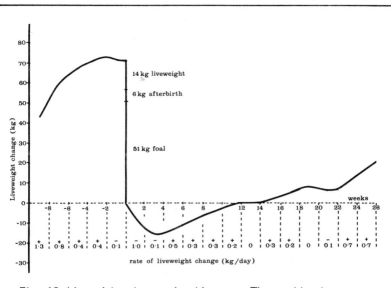

Fig. 18 Liveweight changes in thirty-two Thoroughbred mares before and after foaling.

gradual increase in the digestible energy concentration of the diet during this period — i.e. more grain and less hay should be fed. This probably accounts for the loss in liveweight observed in foaling mares about two weeks before parturition.

The protein requirement of the foetus, above maintenance during the last ninety days of pregnancy, is related to the liveweight of the mare. For mares weighing less than 450 kg. it is assumed to be 1.81 per cent of their body weight; for mares weighing 450 kg. and over it is given as 1.51 per cent of body weight[1]. (See Fig. 17.) When this is expressed in terms of percentage crude protein in the ration, the following figures are advised:

First 250 days
    of gestation . . . . . . . . .8.5 per cent CP on DM basis
Last 90 days
    of gestation . . . . . . . .11.0 per cent CP on DM basis

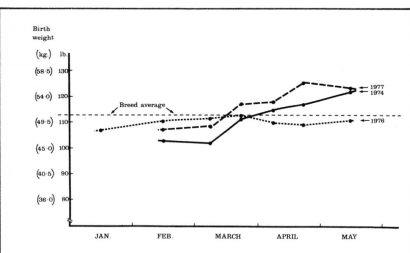

Fig. 19 Birth weights of 261 Thoroughbred foals arranged on a monthly basis.

Larger mares require a greater quantity of food per day, which automatically increases the weight of protein consumed. In-foal and lactating mares have a critical requirement for protein quality. A deficiency of essential amino acids may result in the birth of smaller than average foals or reduced milk yields. Spring grass is a readily available source of energy, essential amino acids, minerals, vitamins and unidentified factors, capable of rectifying deficiencies in traditional oat, bran and hay diets. It is suggested this may account for the seasonal rise in birth weight of foals and the absence of such a rise in 1976 (a drought year).

The mare's greatest requirement for dietary energy and protein occurs *after* foaling and *not* before. Before foaling a condition score of between 2–3 should be maintained, but not exceeded. It is assumed by the NRC that the horse converts digestible energy into milk energy with 60 per cent efficiency[1]. For every kg. of milk produced, 3.3 MJ of digestible energy are required.

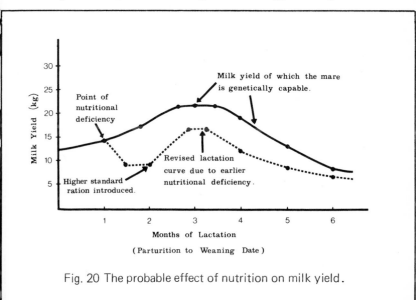

Fig. 20 The probable effect of nutrition on milk yield.

Estimated milk yield at peak lactation is shown below, expressed as a percentage of liveweight.

| Liveweight (kg.) | Estimated peak yield (kg./day) | % of liveweight |
|---|---|---|
| 200 | 10 | 5.0 |
| 250 | 12.5 | 5.0 |
| 300 | 15 | 5.0 |
| 350 | 17 | 4.8 |
| 400 | 18 | 4.5 |
| 500 | 20 | 4.0 |
| 600 | 24 | 4.0 |

With reference to the lactation curve shown in Fig. 20, and to Fig. 27 in the next chapter, it can be seen that demand for protein and energy is highest for the first three months or so of lactation and gradually falls to weaning. A high-protein/high-energy diet must be used in early lactation if the mare's full potential is to be realised. Where digestible energy requirement is not met, there is excessive weight loss and milk yield may fall. If a higher standard ration is introduced later, milk yield rises but never quite reaches the mare's full genetic potential. Excessive weight loss after calving is known to have an adverse effect on fertility in cattle, and the same is probably true for horses. An investigation involving fifteen lactating mares showed that conception is more likely to occur during a period of weight gain. This is not offered as a solution to infertility problems – in most cases other factors are involved – but it obviously helps. It has long been recognised that barren and maiden mares in rising condition are easier to get in foal.

The mare's protein requirement is given as:

First 3 months
of lactation . . . . . . . . 14 per cent CP on DM basis
From 3 months
to weaning. . . . . . . . . 12 per cent CP on DM basis[1]

| Mare | Day covered after foaling | Weight change at time of covering (kg/day) | Result of PD |
|:---:|:---:|:---:|:---:|
| 1 | 42 | +0·3 | + |
| 2 | 100 | −0·3 | − |
| 3 | 30 | +0·5 | + |
| 4 | 43 | +1·1 | + |
| 5 | 10 | −2·3 | − |
| 5 | 60 | +0·3 | + |
| 6 | 34 | +0·9 | + |
| 7 | 8 | −1·3 | − |
| 7 | 48 | +1·1 | + |
| 8 | 40 | +0·9 | + |
| 9 | 33 | +0·4 | + |
| 10 | 26 | +1·9 | + |
| 11 | 26 | +0·3 | − |
| 11 | 46 | +0·3 | + |
| 12 | 26 | +0·4 | + |
| 13 | 27 | −0·3 | − |
| 13 | 49 | +0·3 | + |
| 14 | 27 | +3·3 | + |
| 15 | 28 | +0·9 | + |

Fig. 21 Relationship between liveweight change and conception in fifteen lactating mares.

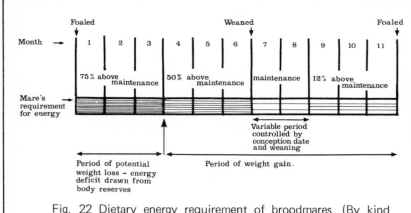

Fig. 22 Dietary energy requirement of broodmares. (By kind permission of the NRC[1].)

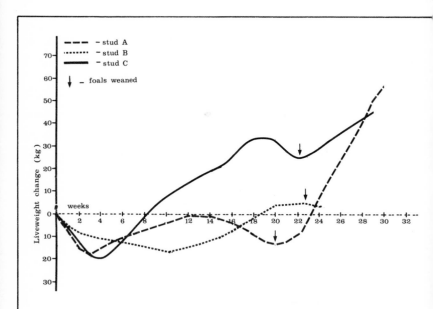

Fig. 23 Effect of individual management on liveweight change after foaling. (Data from thirty-two Thoroughbred mares.)

The effect of milk yield on demand for protein and energy is clearly demonstrated in Figs. 16 and 17. Whereas pregnancy increases demand by 12 per cent, lactation almost doubles the maintenance demand.

Some weight loss after foaling is inevitable, but this should be controlled by nutrition. During the last ninety days of pregnancy and throughout lactation mares consume three per cent of their body weight in food per day. Initially appetite cannot accommodate the mare's digestible energy requirement — that is, it is impossible to formulate a ration containing enough megajoules (MJ) of digestible energy (DE) in the number of kg. or lb. the mare can eat each day — so the energy deficit is drawn from the mare's body reserves. As lactation advances, so demand for nutrients falls. It matches and then eventually exceeds supply and weight is gained. If the supply of dietary energy never exceeds demand, milk yield will fall, enabling liveweight to stabilise, and the mare will remain in poor condition throughout lactation.

The lower the level of nutrition, the longer weight gain will be delayed. In Fig. 23 it can be observed that there was an average 28 kg. difference at twelve weeks post partum in the weight gained by the mares on stud C as compared with those on stud B. Fig. 14 shows the analysis of hay fed on these studs that year and should be compared with the mares' liveweight change. The mares on studs A and C were turned out night and day by twelve weeks after foaling. Those on stud B continued to come in each night until weaning. Once out, the mares on stud A were not offered a supplementary ration. A generally higher level of nutrition based on better hay resulted in a turn round in liveweight change by day 22. Where the ration was based on low-energy hay and the mares were stabled each night throughout the summer, weight loss continued until day seventy.

Increasingly, Thoroughbred mares with foals at foot are turned out to grass day and night once the weather is warmer and the foals are about six weeks old. Whereas

foals are often creep fed, mares are seldom offered concentrates at this time but rely solely on the available
herbage. A survey involving eleven Thoroughbred mares
indicated that supplementary feeding at this time may
be desirable if weight loss is to be avoided. Only three
mares maintained their weight gain on being turned out.
This was: +1.0; +1.1; +1.7 kg./day. The remaining eight
mares lost weight at the rate of: three at −0.2 kg./day;
two at −1.1 kg./day and one each at −0.4, −0.5 and
−1.9 kg./day. The average for the whole group gave a
daily weight loss of −0.2 kg./day.

The difference in weight change between the individuals underlines the fact that mares can differ greatly in
terms of appetite, milk yield and therefore demand for
nutrient density in their rations i.e. the number of MJ
of DE; kg. CP (crude protein) etc. it contains. So weight
changes should be recorded and used to identify individuals needing special care. From a comparison of
Figs. 17 and 29 it can be seen that the lactating mare's
requirement for energy is related to her milk production
and in terms of quantity is higher than that of her foal.
From one to three months of age half the foal's protein
and energy requirement is met by milk.

Since mares in rising condition are easier to get in
foal, it is suggested they should be fed to stop weight loss
by the second heat period (one month after foaling),
with feeding continued for steady gain throughout lactation and pregnancy to include:
 (1)  Replacement of lost condition,
 (2)  Milk yield,
 (3)  Growth of the unborn foal and afterbirth.

Foals are usually weaned at six months old. If the
mare is covered at her foaling heat (seven to ten days
post-partum) and holds, i.e. remains in-foal, the foetus
can also be six months old at this time. A foal born in
April may be weaned in October while the mare remains
at grass until November, at a time of low nutritional
value. She foals again in March (eleven months). This

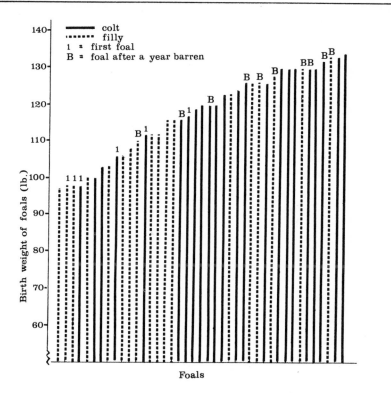

Fig. 24 Birth weights of forty-one Thoroughbred foals.

gives her two months during late autumn and early winter in which to 'recharge her batteries' before entering the period of maximum foetal growth. Traditionally, weight gain is left until the last ninety days of pregnancy when condition, in the long term, is bound to suffer. At this time the mare gives priority to the needs of the foal she is carrying and its afterbirth. This is probably the reason why foals born after a year barren tend to be heavier at birth than average for the breed. Since it is economically unsound to breed from mares in alter-

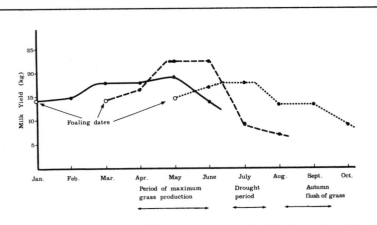

Fig. 25 Probable lactation curves of mares foaling in early, mid and late season.

nate years, their nutritional needs must be studied throughout lactation and pregnancy to achieve optimum results.

As there is no spring grass most years until March, early foalers rely entirely on hay and concentrates for their nutrient requirements and miss most of the benefits of spring grass as a means of boosting milk yield and weight gain. The grass comes too late to affect peak production but does tend to maintain the yield for a longer period, which must be borne in mind when weaning early foals at a time of maximum grass growth.

Spring grass boosts the yield of mares foaling in mid-season, and their milk yield will have dropped by weaning time. This foaling period allows maximum use of available grass and represents the greatest economy.

Those foaling in late season will miss the benefits of spring grass beyond early lactation and should be offered additional concentrates throughout peak production, especially if this period coincides with a drought. See Fig. 23, stud A weeks twelve to eighteen.

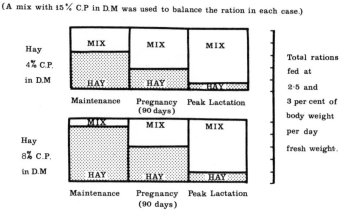

Fig. 26 Examples showing the ratio of concentrates to hay for broodmares using forage of different protein values.

Although a mare in the last ninety days of pregnancy may derive adequate nutrients from spring grass alone, she should be offered additional concentrates in preparation for the diet she will receive after foaling.

A ration identical to those given in Fig. 35 is equally suitable for pregnant and lactating mares. The ratio of mix to hay or grass depends on the individual and value of the hay or grass available.

REFERENCES

1 NRC *Nutrient Requirements of Horses* National Research Council, Washington D.C. **6**, 2, 3, 5, 21 (1978).
2 Ott, E.A. 'Energy and protein for reproduction in the horse' in *Proceedings of the Second Equine Nutritional Symposium*, Cornell Univ., Ithaca, N.Y. pp. 6-10 (1971).

3 Breuer, L.H. 'Effects of mare diet during late gestation and lactation, supplemental feeding of foal and early weaning on foal development' in *Proceedings of the Fourth Equine Nutritional Symposium,* Calif. State Polytech. Univ., Pomona, p. 114 (1975).

# 8 Nutrient Requirements of the Young Horse

The young foal's nutrient requirements are initially met by mare's milk alone. The time a foal takes to suck after birth varies between 35 and 420 minutes, with a mean time of 111 minutes[1]. Most find the teats on their own and are confused by the well-intentioned help of attendants, but a very few weak foals require assistance. Some maiden mares need to be held or restrained before they will allow a foal to suck.

Foals are born with no antibodies against disease in their blood; these are obtained in massive doses from colostrum (first milk) and absorbed through the small intestine for a brief period (less than thirty-six hours) after birth. Foals must therefore receive a supply of mare's colostrum within the first twenty-four hours of birth if they are to acquire resistance to disease. Mares which have run their milk before foaling may have no colostrum by the time the foal arrives. In these cases an alternative supply must be found. Deep-frozen colostrum will keep for a year.

While colostrum is very high in protein, there is a steep fall in protein, gross energy, specific gravity and total solids within twelve hours of birth and a steady fall through to four months of lactation (see Fig. 27)[2]. Lactose (milk sugar) and butterfat increase over the same period. Phosphorus concentration rises from birth to forty-eight hours and then declines. Calcium drops for twelve hours before rising to a peak at eight days and then gradually declines. Levels of magnesium, potassium, and sodium fall over the first four months of lactation.

Most milk constituents are synthesised in the mammary gland from precursors available in the mare's

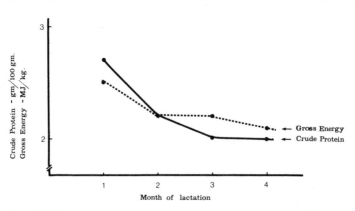

Fig. 27 Changes in gross energy and crude protein composition of mare's milk between one and four months of lactation. (After Ullrey, D.E. *et al*.)

blood, or by straightforward transfer of nutrients, as in the case of vitamins and minerals. The mare's nutritional status is therefore reflected in her milk.

About 95 per cent of milk nitrogen is present as protein and about 78 per cent of this is casein. Amino acids are absorbed by the mammary gland and converted into protein. Lactose is the only carbohydrate in milk apart from traces of glucose and galactose. Butterfat is a mixture of triglycerides and a range of unsaturated fatty acids. Mares have a lower butterfat level than other species of farm animal, normally not exceeding 2 per cent.

Milk contains the major elements, calcium, phosphorus, sodium, potassium, magnesium and chlorine, and also very small amounts of certain trace elements, assuming these are present in the mare's blood. Their presence in milk may have an important bearing on the health of the foal. The mammary gland shows considerable selectivity and will block the entry of some elements in favour of others. This can be a disadvantage, notably in the case of iron and copper. Both elements are essential for haemoglobin formation, yet their level in milk cannot be raised no matter how much is fed to the mare. However the foal receives a supply of iron from colostrum, which contains fifteen times the amount in normal milk, providing the mare's liver stores are adequate to meet the demand. Older foals should be offered mineral licks containing traces of iron and copper.

Vitamins present in milk include both vitamin A and its precursor beta-carotene, their level depending on the mare's diet. The amounts of C and D are small, while only traces of vitamins E and K occur. A large range of the B vitamins is present, and these compensate for the foal's inability to manufacture its own supply until microbial digestion is established – up to seven months old. To compensate for any shortfall as the milk yield declines and after weaning, dried yeast (about one table-spoonful per foal per day), plus a vitamin $B_{12}$ supplement, should be added to the diet of animals between three and nine months old. Vitamin A and $D_3$ supplements must be included in the diet of all foals, at least until they are receiving enough from natural sources. Where foals are stabled for weaning or during the winter months, vitamins A, $D_3$ and the B-complex as well as a mineral supplement containing enough calcium and/or phosphorus to balance the ration should be included.

The mammary gland must be provided with a wide range of nutrients if it is to function at optimum levels. These are supplied by the diet and/or microbial activity in the large intestine. Any shortfall is likely to affect milk production and therefore growth rate of the foal.

The foal's growth rate is influenced by nutrition and health. For the first week of their lives foals eat little, if any, concentrates, so weight gain is related entirely to milk yield. Thoroughbred foals, with access from birth to a balanced concentrate ration containing high-grade protein, tend to gain weight faster than those receiving

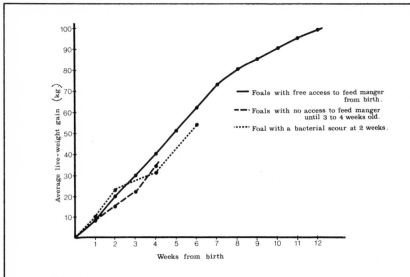

Fig. 28 Average weekly weight gain from birth to twelve weeks.
(Data from twenty-three Thoroughbred foals.)

mare's milk alone up to three to four weeks old. Those introduced to concentrates at the later date then exhibit a faster growth rate and eventually catch up with other foals. There was no significant difference in health between the two groups. Where mares are exhibited or sold with young foals at foot, it is suggested there may be some advantage in creep feeding from birth.

A smooth curve indicates a normal growth pattern, whereas a zigzag line indicates a check in growth rate, as in the case of the scouring foal in Fig. 28 above.

Long mangers should be used in loose-boxes housing mares and foals, and food must be scattered the length of the manger to allow both maximum space to eat. In addition foal creep feeders should be installed: this way optimum growth rate can be maintained.

The mammary gland should be examined twice a day,

i.e. morning before turning out and at night on coming in, to make sure the foal is sucking normally. A full udder indicates that the foal is probably off colour. Sucking time of a normal healthy foal gradually decreases from four times an hour in the first week of life to twice an hour by the sixth week and only once an hour by six months[3]. The udder is therefore kept slack, and any sign of fullness indicates that the foal is 'off-suck'. In order to nurse, the normal procedure is for the foal to move across in front of the mare to stop her, before approaching the udder. The mare terminates sucking by walking off, threatening to kick or bite the foal. As weaning time approaches so contact between mare and foal becomes less and less.

The young foal is thought not to develop a full complement of gut microbes until it is about seven months old. Digestion of fibre is carried out by microbes in the large intestine, so the foal's ability to digest hay gradually improves over the seven months period, as the microbes become established. It is interesting to observe whole pieces of undigested hay in the droppings of very young foals.

Initially energy is provided entirely from lactose and butterfat in milk. This is gradually supplemented with glucose from the breakdown of carbohydrate in grain, then finally with surplus protein and volatile fatty acids produced by the action of gut microbes mainly on fibre. These are the three gradually developing stages, normally complete by seven months, which lead to adult digestion in the foal.

There are four phases in the foal's digestive development towards independence:

(1)  milk diet alone;
(2)  milk + concentrates;
(3)  milk + concentrates + hay;
(4)  concentrates + hay.

Ad lib. hay should be offered from birth to encourage development of microbial digestion.

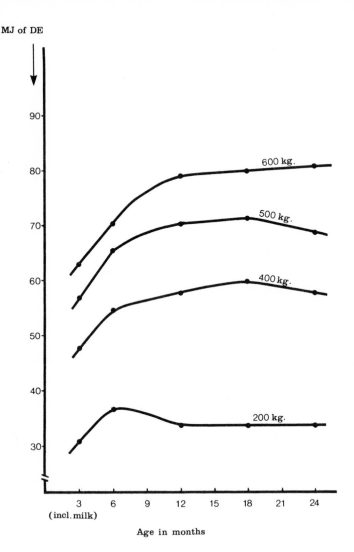

Fig. 29 Dietary energy requirement of youngstock with different mature weights. (By kind permission of the NRC[4].)

Since the young foal is unable to digest fibre efficiently its diet must be based on the very best hay obtainable. Foals are unable to digest sucrose (sugar) efficiently until they are about seven months old and should not be given foods, such as molassed sugar beet pulp, which contain this substance.

Sucrose digestion develops gradually and is considered to be:

30 per cent efficient at birth;

40 per cent efficient by four months:

100 per cent efficient by seven months.

Curves are given in Fig. 29 showing the recommended levels of dietary energy for youngstock from three to twenty-four months old, with different mature weights[4]. The curves reflect rate of growth and development in relation to mature weight. A higher growth potential necessitates a higher-quality diet. Requirement falls as the animal matures.

Energy-deficient youngstock appear in poor condition and are prone to disease. Growing bone is susceptible to damage by injudicious management. For instance, excess dietary energy in foals and yearlings leads to conditions such as epiphysitis or bowed legs, associated with putting too much weight on immature limbs.

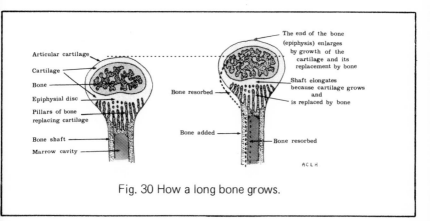

Fig. 30 How a long bone grows.

All bones originate as cartilage. As the foetus develops during the 340 days inside the mare, cartilage is gradually replaced by bone. At the time of birth the process is well advanced but by no means complete. Fig. 30 shows how a long bone grows.

The length of a bone is increased by cartilage cell activity at its ends (epiphyses). Cartilage, unlike bone, is capable of growing larger within itself. Bone can only grow by the addition of new bone onto existing bone.

The epiphysis (growth plate) is composed of cartilage which is gradually replaced by bone as it closes. The degree to which this plate has closed in the various bones of the body is taken as a guide to the animal's physical development at that age. Some bones close long before others — the vertebrae in the horse's back, for

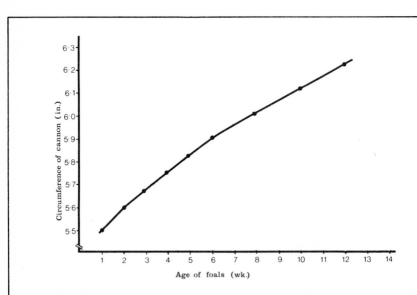

Fig. 31 Average weekly increase in circumference of the cannon bone from birth to twelve weeks. (Data from nineteen Thoroughbred foals.)

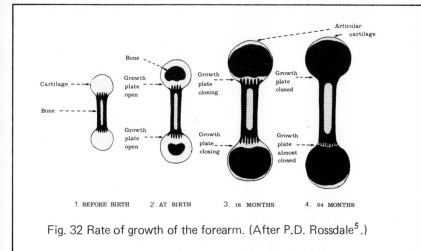

Fig. 32 Rate of growth of the forearm. (After P.D. Rossdale[5].)

example, seldom finish growing before five years old[5]. Those in the pastern close by six to nine months, and at the end of the cannon, where it articulates with the fetlock joint, between nine and twelve months old. The epiphysis at the end of the forearm (radius) where it articulates with the knee joint, does not close until the horse is 24-30 months old. The epiphyses remain open only until growth of the bone is complete. When all epiphyses are closed the horse is fully grown.

Hormones, including the sex hormones, affect rate of closure. It is interesting to note the even growth rate of a group of colts and fillies up to sexual maturity. At that time, testosterone (the male sex hormone) slows down the rate of epiphyseal closure, allowing growth to proceed unchecked. Oestrogen (the female sex hormone), on the other hand, promotes closure and therefore slows down growth rate in the fillies. Lucerne (alfalfa) and extracted soyabean meal contain naturally occurring oestrogens. Anabolic steroids tend to hasten epiphyseal closure. When used to excess they produce well-muscled, stunted animals.

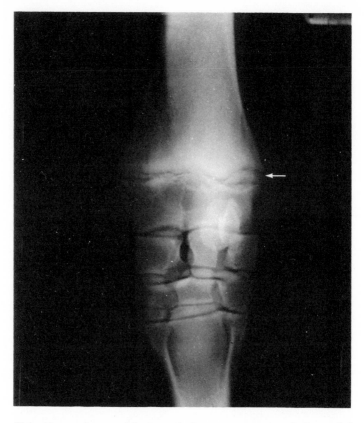

This X-ray shows widening of the outer aspect of the radial (knee) epiphysis caused by an imbalance in the dietary calcium:phosphorus ratio.

Until the leg epiphyses are closed, inflammation (epiphysitis) can occur in susceptible individuals, usually close to the time of epiphyseal closure. That is, immediately above and below the fetlock joint in foals and above the knee in yearlings. The condition is characterised by heat, swelling and pain. It is quite common for only one individual in a large group to be affected. The following appear to be predisposing causes:

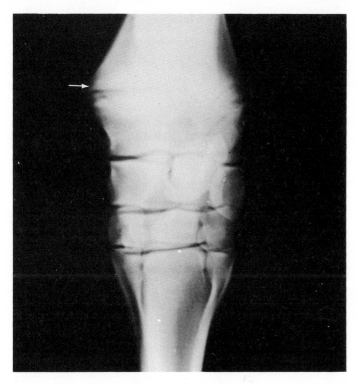

This X-ray shows a reaction on the inside of the knee, the more usual site for inflammation of the radial epiphysis. In this case there is a slight deviation of the epiphysis to the inside, collo-quially known as 'benched knees'.

(1) Heavy topped individuals.
(2) Abnormally fast growth rates.
(3) Possible reduced ability to absorb dietary calcium and phosphorus, or an imbalance of the dietary calcium:phosphorus ratio.
(4) Upright limb conformation.
(5) Hard ground.
(6) Sudden alteration to the bearing surface of the foot, e.g. when a 'toes-out' or 'toes-in' position is corrected too quickly.

Recommended treatment is to reduce the energy level of the ration — if necessary feed hay alone and house on peat moss deep litter. This lessens pressure on the epiphyses. Normal growth continues even at maintenance energy levels. Below maintenance, bone growth may be seriously inhibited[6]. Therefore only good-quality hay should be used. Poor hay would also be deficient in protein, vitamins and minerals. Ensure that there is enough available calcium, phosphorus and vitamin $D_3$ in the diet to satisfy the animal's requirements. Your veterinary surgeon or blacksmith should be consulted to rectify any deviations from normal in the limbs. Those charac-

Epiphysitis

Fig. 33 Epiphysitis in the foal. Foal or yearling up to twelve months old showing upright pasterns and round fetlock joints which are typical of epiphysitis at this age.

teristic of this condition are upright pasterns in foals and a marked 'toes-in' position in yearlings.

Youngstock should therefore be kept on a balanced diet, in moderate but not fat condition (condition score: 1½−2) and maintaining an even growth rate close to optimum for the breed or type. Leg epiphyses should be examined regularly for signs of inflammation.

Up to the age of two years, horses have a critical protein requirement. That is, the amino acid composition of their diet is as important as the percentage protein. Low-protein diets or diets lacking in lysine result in low

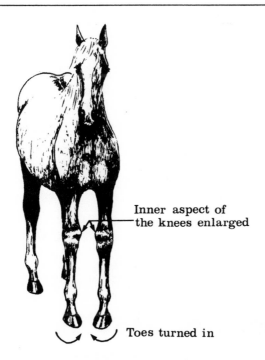

Inner aspect of
the knees enlarged

Toes turned in

Fig. 34 Epiphysitis in the yearling. Yearling or two year old up to thirty months old showing enlargements on the inner aspect of the knees and associated toes-in position.

growth rates, suggesting depressed cell activity at the epiphyses. The quantity of protein needed by young horses depends on the amino acid composition of the diet. Low-quality dietary protein necessitates a higher quantity to achieve satisfactory results. Excess protein is converted to carbohydrate and stored as fat, leading to overweight and possible epiphysitis. The requirement for all essential amino acids is not known, but it is known that weaned foals under twelve months old require 0.6-0.7 per cent lysine[7].

The histograms below show the essential amino acid breakdown of five similar diets using different sources of protein. The dotted lines indicate the recommended lysine level. The diets containing extracted soyabean meal and fish meal are therefore the most satisfactory in this case for foals and yearlings.

The following protein allowances, expressed as a percentage of the total diet, are recommended[4]:

*Foals*: 18 per cent CP but gradually dropping to 16 per cent CP by the time they are six months old;

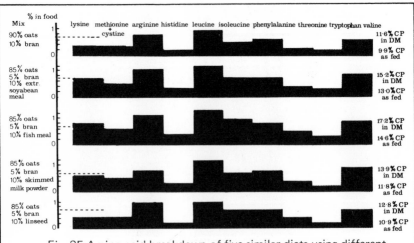

Fig. 35 Amino acid breakdown of five similar diets using different sources of protein.

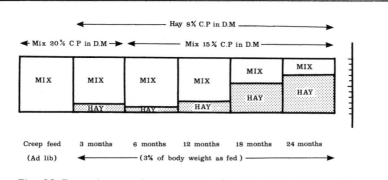

Fig. 36 Examples showing the ratio of concentrates to hay for young horses up to twenty-four months old.

*Weaned foals*: 16 per cent CP gradually dropping to 13.5 per cent CP by the time they are a year old;

*Yearlings*: 13.5 per cent CP gradually dropping to 11 per cent CP by eighteen months old and down to 10 per cent CP by the time they are two-year-olds.

Youngstock consume an average 3 per cent of their body weight in food per day. Therefore their requirement for nutrients must be met within the bounds of this 3 per cent limit. Initially it is necessary to ignore any hay the foal may eat, but by three months old some may be included in the calculation. The ratio of hay to mix is gradually increased over the ensuing period until a ration comprising 60 per cent hay:40 per cent mix (depending on the quality of the hay) can be fed by the time the animal is two years old. Examples showing the ratio of concentrates to hay for young horses up to this age are shown in Fig. 36 above.

REFERENCES

1 Rossdale, P.D. and Ricketts, S.W. *The Practice of Equine Stud Veterinary Medicine,* pub. Bailliere and Tindall **4**, 200 (1974).

2  Ullrey, D.E. *et al.* 'Composition of Mares' Milk' *J. Anim. Sci.* **25**, 217 (1966).

3  Tyler, S.J. 'The Behaviour and Social Organisation of the New Forest Ponies' *Anim. Behav. Monogr.* **5**, 2 (1972).

4  NRC *Nutrient Requirements of Horses* National Research Council **6**, 17-20 (1978).

5  Rossdale, P.D. and Ricketts, S.W. *The Practice of Equine Stud Veterinary Medicine*, pub. Bailliere and Tindall **5**, 298 (1974).

6  Hintz, H.F. and Schryver, H.F. 'Nutrition and Bone Development in Horses' *J. Am. Vet. Med. Asscn.* **168**, 39 (1976).

7  Breuer, L.H., Kasten, L.H. and Word, J.D. 'Protein and Amino Acid Utilization in the Young Horse' in *Proceedings of the Second Equine Nutritional Symposium,* Cornell Univ., 16-17 (1971).

# APPENDIX 1:

# Composition of Foodstuffs

AMINO ACID COMPOSITION OF THE PROTEIN IN FOODSTUFFS COMMONLY INCLUDED IN HORSE RATIONS (To obtain percentage of amino acid in protein, multiply by percentage of protein in individual sample.)

| g. amino acid/16 g total N minus NO$_3$-N | Bran | Oats | Barley | Corn (maize) | Extracted soya-bean meal | White fish meal | Dried skimmed milk | Field beans | Linseed (flax) | Dried yeast | Dried grass* | Dried clover* | Dried lucerne (alfalfa)* | Dried sugar beet pulp |
|---|---|---|---|---|---|---|---|---|---|---|---|---|---|---|
| Lysine | 4.0 | 3.6 | 4.6 | 2.4 | 6.6 | 7.0 | 7.8 | 5.9 | 3.4 | 7.8 | 5.8 | 6.1 | 6.4 | 7.5 |
| Methionine | 1.4 | 1.8 | 1.6 | 1.9 | 1.4 | 2.7 | 2.9 | 0.9 | 1.4 | 1.6 | 2.2 | 1.7 | 1.8 | 0.1 |
| Histidine | 2.0 | 1.6 | 2.0 | 2.1 | 2.7 | 3.1 | 2.5 | 2.3 | 1.9 | 2.8 | 2.2 | 2.5 | 2.5 | 2.5 |
| Arginine | 7.2 | 7.2 | 4.3 | 5.8 | 7.8 | 6.8 | 3.3 | 8.5 | 8.1 | 5.3 | 6.0 | 6.0 | 5.9 | 3.7 |
| Threonine | 3.2 | 2.5 | 3.1 | 3.8 | 3.7 | 4.2 | 5.3 | 3.8 | 3.4 | 5.3 | 4.8 | 4.8 | 4.9 | 5.0 |
| Valine | 4.7 | 5.6 | 5.4 | 4.7 | 5.6 | 5.3 | 7.2 | 4.7 | 4.7 | 6.0 | 6.3 | 6.4 | 6.2 | 5.0 |
| Isoleucine | 4.0 | 4.8 | 3.6 | 4.1 | 5.2 | 5.0 | 6.3 | 3.9 | 5.3 | 6.0 | 4.8 | 4.9 | 5.0 | 3.7 |
| Leucine | 6.0 | 8.1 | 6.9 | 11.2 | 7.6 | 7.4 | 10.0 | 6.2 | 5.9 | 7.2 | 8.8 | 9.0 | 8.9 | 7.5 |
| Phenylalanine | 3.8 | 5.6 | 5.4 | 4.9 | 4.9 | 4.5 | 3.3 | 6.2 | 4.3 | 6.2 | 5.9 | 5.9 | 6.0 | 3.7 |
| Tryptophan | 2.0 | 1.6 | 1.8 | 1.0 | 1.6 | 1.1 | 1.3 | 0.9 | 1.4 | 1.0 | 1.8 | 1.5 | 2.1 | 2.2 |
| Cystine | 2.0 | 1.9 | 2.2 | 1.4 | 1.5 | 1.2 | 1.3 | 1.0 | 1.7 | 1.2 | 1.3 | 1.0 | 1.3 | 0.1 |

* Source: W.H. Eppendorfer J. Sci. Fd. Agric. 28, 612 (1977).

A GUIDE TO THE NUTRITIVE VALUE OF SOME COMMON FOODS

| | Dry matter % | Crude protein % | Digestible crude protein % | Oil % | Crude fibre % | Digestible energy MJ/kg. | Total digestible nutrients % | Calcium % | Phosphorus % | Carotene mg./kg. | COMMENTS |
|---|---|---|---|---|---|---|---|---|---|---|---|
| **CEREALS** | | | | | | | | | | | |
| Oats | 86 | 11 | 8 | 4.9 | 12 | 14 | 73 | 0.09 | 0.37 | 0.1 | When cooked digestible energy is raised by about 3 per cent. |
| Barley | 86 | 11 | 8 | 1.7 | 5 | 16 | 83 | 0.05 | 0.38 | 0.4 | |
| Maize (corn) | 86 | 10 | 8 | 4.2 | 2 | 17 | 90 | 0.01 | 0.27 | 3.4 | |
| **PROTEINS OF ANIMAL ORIGIN** | | | | | | | | | | | |
| White fish meal | 90 | 66 | 60 | 4.0 | 0 | 13 | 70 | 8.0 | 4.0 | — | Correct degree of heat treatment of all proteins important. Heat damage possible during processing. |
| Dried skimmed milk | 90 | 36 | 36 | 0.5 | 0 | 17 | 98 | 1.0 | 0.8 | — | Ability to digest lactose is low after three years old. |
| Dried yeast | 90 | 44 | 38 | 1.0 | 0 | 14 | 76 | 0.2 | 2.8 | — | Abundant source of B-complex vitamins except for $B_{12}$ |
| **VEGETABLE PROTEINS** | | | | | | | | | | | |
| Extracted soyabean meal | 90 | 50 | 45 | 1.0 | 6 | 17 | 82 | 0.25 | 0.60 | 0.2 | Contains trypsin inhibitor if not heat treated. Reduces peptide digestion (see p. 32) |
| Linseed (flax) | 90 | 26 | 21 | 39.0 | 6 | 24 | 88 | 0.30 | 0.58 | — | Can contain a glycoside and its associated enzyme rendering it poisonous under warm, damp or wet conditions, if not heat treated. |
| Field beans | 86 | 25 | 21 | 1.5 | 9 | 15 | 83 | 0.19 | 0.67 | — | Contain low levels of trypsin inhibitor unless cooked, although often fed raw. |

A GUIDE TO THE NUTRITIVE VALUE OF SOME COMMON FOODS

| | Dry matter % | Crude protein % | Digestible crude protein % | Oil % | Crude fibre % | Digestible energy MJ/kg. | Total digestible nutrients % | Calcium % | Phosphorus % | Carotene mg./kg. | COMMENTS |
|---|---|---|---|---|---|---|---|---|---|---|---|
| **ON DRY MATTER (DM) BASIS** | | | | | | | | | | | |
| **INTERMEDIATE FOODS** | | | | | | | | | | | |
| Bran (wheat) | 88 | 17 | 13 | 4.5 | 12 | 12 | 67 | 0.16 | 0.84 | 2.9 | Excess bran produces low calcium uptake leading to calcium:phosphorus imbalance. |
| Grass meal | 90 | 18 | 13 | 3.0 | 18 | 13 | 72 | 0.90 | 0.30 | 200 | Must be dampened or fed as nuts; carotene content declines with storage. |
| Lucerne meal | 90 | 21 | 16 | 3.0 | 20 | 11 | 62 | 1.40 | 0.20 | 200 | |
| Carrots | 13 | 9 | 6 | 1.5 | 11 | 15 | 82 | 0.59 | 0.34 | 800 | High water content may limit intake if fed at high levels. |
| Dried molassed sugar beet pulp | 90 | 10 | 6 | 0.5 | 15 | 14 | 79 | 0.63 | 0.07 | – | Must be soaked overnight before feeding. Foals under seven months old have a reduced ability to digest sucrose (see page 91). |
| **CONSERVED FORAGES** | | | | | | | | | | | |
| Grass hay (good) | 85 | 10 | 6 | 1.6 | 32 | 8 | 62 | 0.40 | 0.25 | 20.0 | Carotene content declines with storage. Vitamin D content depends on length of exposure of cut herbage to the sun. Calcium and phosphorus content of hay and grass meal depends on soil status – figures may be reduced by up to 70 per cent. |
| Grass hay (medium) | 85 | 8 | 4 | 1.6 | 33 | 8 | 57 | 0.38 | 0.21 | 12.0 | |
| Grass hay (poor) | 85 | 4 | 1 | 1.6 | 34 | 9 | 48 | 0.30 | 0.20 | 5.0 | |
| Clover hay | 85 | 13 | 6 | 2.5 | 34 | 9 | 52 | 1.20 | 0.25 | 7.0 | |
| Lucerne hay | 85 | 17 | 11 | 3.1 | 36 | 10 | 53 | 1.80 | 0.30 | 15.0 | |
| Silage (grass) | 25 | 16 | 10 | 3.5 | 34 | 11 | 60 | 0.65 | 0.35 | 22.0 | |

VITAMIN A REQUIREMENT

|  | IU/kg. |
|---|---|
| Mature horses and ponies (work does not increase requirement) | 1,600 |
| Mare, last 90 days of gestation | 3,400 |
| Lactating mare, first 3 months | 2,800 |
| Lactating mare, 3 months to weaning | 2,450 |
| Youngstock from birth to 2 years old | 2,000 |

*Source*: NRC *Nutrient Requirements of Horses* **6**, 21 (1978).

# APPENDIX 2:
## Weight Equivalents

IMPERIAL/METRIC WEIGHT EQUIVALENTS

1 lb.  ~453.6 g.  ~0.4536 kg.  ~16 oz.
1 oz.  ~28.35 g.
1 kg.  ~1,000 g.  ~2.2046 lb.
1 g.  ~1,000 mg.
1 mg.  ~1,000 $\mu$g. ~0.001 g.
1 $\mu$g.  ~0.001 mg.~0.000 001 g.
1 $\mu$g. per g. or 1 mg. per kg. or 1 g. per tonne is the same as p.p.m.

WEIGHT-UNIT CONVERSION FACTORS

| Units given | Units wanted | For conversion multiply by: |
|---|---|---|
| lb. | g. | 453.6 |
| lb. | kg. | 0.4536 |
| oz. | g. | 28.35 |
| kg. | lb. | 2.2046 |
| kg. | mg. | 1,000,000 |
| kg. | g. | 1,000 |
| g. | mg. | 1,000 |
| mg/g. | mg./lb. | 453.6 |
| mg./kg. | mg./lb. | 0.4536 |
| Mcal. | kcal. | 1,000 |
| kcal./kg. | kcal./lb. | 0.4536 |
| kcal./lb. | kcal./kg. | 2.2046 |
| p.p.m. | mg./kg. | 1.0 |
| p.p.m. | mg./lb. | 0.4536 |
| mg./kg. | per cent | 0.0001 |
| p.p.m. | per cent | 0.0001 |
| mg./g. | per cent | 0.1 |
| g./kg. | per cent | 0.1 |
| kcal./kg. | MJ/kg. | divide by 1,000 then multiply by 4.2 |
| to convert air dry to DM (dry matter) | | divide by 0.88 |

# APPENDIX 3:
## Weight Estimation Tables

TABLE SHOWING THE NON-ADJUSTED WEIGHT ESTIMATION
FACTOR Y FOR USE WITH THE FORMULA GIVEN ON PAGE 18

| THOROUGHBREDS | | | NON-THOROUGHBREDS | |
|---|---|---|---|---|
| FEMALES | MALES | GELDINGS | FEMALES | GELDINGS |
| 306.6 | 295.3 | 298.0 | 293.1 | 292.6 |

The above table should only be used where, for some
reason, the horse's condition score cannot be obtained.
In all other cases refer to the table on page 107.

TABLE GIVING THE ADJUSTED FACTOR Y ACCORDING TO CONDITION SCORE FOR EACH CLASS OF HORSE OR PONY FOR USE WITH THE FORMULA GIVEN ON PAGE 18.

| Condition Score | CLASS OF ANIMAL | | | | |
|---|---|---|---|---|---|
| | TB FEMALE | TB MALE | TB GELDING | NON-TB FEMALE | NON-TB GELDING |
| 0 | 328.4 | 323.1 | 327.0 | 316.9 | 324.2 |
| 0.5 | 324.6 | 318.0 | 322.1 | 313.9 | 319.2 |
| 1.0 | 320.8 | 313.0 | 317.2 | 311.0 | 314.3 |
| 1.5 | 317.0 | 308.0 | 312.3 | 308.0 | 309.3 |
| 2.0 | 313.2 | 302.9 | 307.5 | 305.1 | 304.4 |
| 2.5 | 309.4 | 297.9 | 302.6 | 302.1 | 299.5 |
| 3.0 | 305.6 | 292.8 | 297.7 | 299.2 | 294.5 |
| 3.5 | 301.8 | 287.8 | 292.8 | 296.2 | 289.6 |
| 4.0 | 298.0 | 282.8 | 287.9 | 293.3 | 284.6 |
| 4.5 | 294.2 | 277.7 | 283.1 | 290.3 | 279.7 |
| 5.0 | 291.4 | 272.7 | 278.2 | 287.4 | 274.8 |

*Source:* Leighton Hardman A.C. 'Study of the Relationship Between Body Measurement, Body Condition and Liveweight of the Horse' (1981).

# Conclusion

Most horse owners tend to overfeed their animals, although a few consistently underfeed. Efficient owners recognise the link between nutrition, condition, optimum weight, health and performance. Others, who are less conscientious, fail to note their horse's condition or observe changes in it. A method of weight estimation based on condition scoring makes the operator aware of this important facet of management. This in itself is an advantage and could reduce the incidence of obesity-related disease conditions.

The keeping of regular weight records improves management efficiency on studs and in stables. They may be used to maintain an even growth rate in young stock and condition scoring would help to reduce the incidence of epiphysitis.

To facilitate early conception, broodmares should be weighed, or their weight estimated, on a regular basis. This would have an economic advantage as keep charges on most public studs are high.

Trainers, over the years, have found that each horse has an individual optimum or racing weight which co-incides with peak performance. Once this optimum weight has been established, any weight loss occurring after a competitive event should be made good before the next outing. This is of particular importance when an animal competes or is raced over a long season. Such a system of management reduces the incidence of over or under feeding and is applicable to all forms of equestrian activity.

# Index